# KENNETH C. ULMER
# WALLS
# CAN FALL

# KENNETH C. ULMER

# WALLS CAN FALL

## Race, Reconciliation & Righteousness in a Divided World

Published by Carver House
ISBN: 978-0-578-59381-4

For foreign and subsidiary rights, contact the author.

Cover designed by Derrick Pete.

Developmental edit by M. Rutledge McCall

# ENDORSEMENTS

## Walls Can Fall

"...seeks to speak into the racial fatigue that blacks are feeling and the seeming lack of progress with race relations in spite of eight years of a black presidency and multiple book volumes, talks, films... Ongoing police killings of unarmed black people, racial insults raining down from the Executive Branch of the government, gentrification, redlining, voter suppression, and the ongoing trauma of being black in America ...Bishop Ulmer urges us to return to the Holy Book for answers. Taking a practical, biblical and theological approach, injected with humor and personal anecdotes, Walls Can Fall brings into plain view God's big picture for humanity...."

—**Dr. Clifton Clarke,** Fuller Theological Seminary; Pasadena, California

## A FEW COMMENTS ON OTHER BOOKS BY KENNETH C. ULMER

## Passing The Generation Blessings

"Embracing the ideas in this book requires unselfishness and a willingness to prepare yourself so you can help others prepare.... to pay the lessons forward so the next generation wouldn't have to experience the trials and tribulations that you did.... I've learned to put aside my ego [and] drop the façade. Are you willing to step aside and take a back seat in order to bless the younger generations with the wisdom, insight, and experience you've gained? ...The principles in this book, the stories in this book, are a challenge to you and me... to make wise decisions moving forward...to embolden us to live out

*our own personal stories to the fullest.... Are you going to let the past hold your future hostage?"*
—**LL Cool J,** Actor, "NCIS: Los Angeles"; Rapper, two-time Grammy Award Winner, Kennedy Center Honoree

*"In this insightful work, my good friend Dr. Kenneth Ulmer challenges, encourages, and convicts us about the absolute necessity of providing a spiritual legacy for the next generation. Passing the Generation Blessing will equip God's people to fight and win the battle for ourselves and for those who are looking to us to victoriously guide them into the future of God's blessing."*
—**Dr. Tony Evans**, President, The Urban Alternative; Senior pastor, Oak Cliff Bible Fellowship

*"Challenging. Provoking. Encouraging. Biblical. Hopeful. Wow! These are some of my first responses to Passing the Generation Blessing by my friend Bishop Kenneth Ulmer. His ability to translate ancient biblical texts into twenty-first-century parlance is unparalleled. However, what I love most about this book is that the messenger is the message. Bishop Ulmer's internal personal congruence is personified in this book. You'll learn, grow, and share this with all Christian leaders you know—I did."*
—**Sam Chand,** Author, Leadership Consultant

*"An inheritance is lost and succession broken when the impartation of those who have journeyed well is not carefully bestowed upon capable sons and daughters. Equally as distressing is the reality of successors who dismiss the lasting value in the wisdom and blessing of well-seasoned leaders. Dr. Kenneth C. Ulmer, in Passing the Generation Blessing, builds a masterful case for intergenerational continuity and revives the mandate for us to not only 'run well' but to 'finish well.'"*
—**Wayne Chaney, Jr.,** Senior Pastor, Antioch Church of Long Beach, California

"*From the many books written by Dr. Kenneth Ulmer, a prolific speaker, author, and scholar, I find none more compelling or important to the believer than this new release, Passing the Generation Blessing. With more than fifty years of ministry experience, one of my greatest heartbreaks is to see how few leaders pass a legacy to the next generation. Pastors rarely prepare for their successor, dads fail to bless their children, church leaders build ministries without making disciples, and the next generation waits for someone to pass them the baton ...but they wait in vain. This book will ignite a new passion that will drive you to biblical, Spirit-filled action. Bless and empower the next generation before it's too late.*"

—**Larry Titus**, President, Kingdom Global Ministries

"*Kenneth Ulmer takes you through a transformative path to partner with the next generation by passing on a godly legacy. He is a prolific writer, leader, pastor, and brother in Christ. Our partnership stems from our history with Empowered21, a network of global ministries addressing the challenges of the Spirit-empowered church in the twenty-first century. Passing the Generation Blessing is a much-needed resource that will benefit both parents and children. The practical stories and history that flow forth from this book will enrich your life far beyond the time you spend reading them and will help you further engrain many of life's lessons God shares with us in His Word.*"

—**Ossie Mills,** Vice President of Communications and Marketing, Oral Roberts University; Executive Director, Empowered21

"*This generation is longing to be fathered, mentored, and nurtured by those who have walked under a grace and favor that must be released so that generations to come will fulfill the call on their lives. Passing the Generation Blessing is a seminal work that must be read by all who lead in this milieu.*"

—**Jody Moore,** Senior Pastor, Praise Tabernacle Bible Church, Chino, California

*"Why do organizations and nations gradually decline over time? Why is it that the first generation generates; the second generation, motivates; the third generation, speculates; and the fourth generation dissipates? The leadership answer is found in how the leader passes the baton of blessing to the next generation. In Passing the Generation Blessing, Dr. Kenneth Ulmer clearly explains how to pass the leadership blessing to the generations that follow for multipliable and maximized success! Dr. Ulmer teaches us how to prepare, plan, and process for 'generational wins!'"*

**—Dr. James O. Davis**, Founder and President, Cutting Edge International Global Church Network, Orlando, Florida

*"Often times as followers of Christ, many of us lose our way. We lose our identity. We lose our purpose. In his new book, Passing the Generation Blessing, my dear brother Bishop Ken Ulmer points us to the way back and the way up by clearly illuminating our path to be blessed and to be a blessing. Today the world is ever so lost and broken. What is to come for the next generation? We are all called to the way of truth and righteousness by passing on the generation blessing. Thank you, Bishop Ulmer, for writing this powerful and anointed treatise, and may God be glorified in all we do."*

**—Frank Sontag**, Founder, KMG Ministries

*"I have been great friends with Ken for many years, and I believe God has uniquely gifted him to make the Bible relevant in every area of our lives. In his new book, Passing the Generation Blessing, he explains how important it is for us to share the stories about God's work in our lives, because our testimonies can change lives. If you want to have an impact on the next generation, you have to tell your story!"*

**—Robert Morris**, Best-selling author; Lead Senior Pastor, Gateway Church

"*For the better part of my life I have had a front-row seat to view the faithfulness of God as both told and modeled by the life and ministry of my godfather, Bishop Kenneth Ulmer. What he writes in this book, he has done for me—passed the baton. Bishop Ulmer is not entering the winter years of his life as some curmudgeon, but as a godly patriarch who is leveraging the odometer of his life to invest in the coming generations for a time he will not see. Reading Passing the Generation Blessing, you will be inspired to tell your story!*"
—**Bryan Loritts,** Author, Senior Pastor, Abundant Life Christian Fellowship, Mountain View, California

"*In Dr. Kenneth Ulmer's new book, Passing the Generation Blessing, the theme addresses an essential value that every family should embrace, and the author is a leader who has modeled this message in his ministry, marriage, and home. Ken is a personal friend, in whom I can fully attest to the depth of his character, strength of his ministry, verification of his ability, and the fruitful impact of his ministry in Los Angeles, across the United States, and in nations of the world where he has ministered.*"
—**Jack W. Hayford,** President, Foursquare Churches International; Chancellor, The King's College and Seminary; Founding Pastor, The Church On The Way

"*This teaching of the urgency of passing this generation's blessings, lessons, and accumulated wisdom and experiences to the next generation, is one of the most crucial and timely works of the new millennium— particularly in light of the state of affairs of this present generation.... Pastor Ulmer is in a rarified echelon of leaders, professors, pastors, and teachers who truly 'get it.' He not only has the heart of the Lord, but he is uniquely gifted at 'unpacking,' disseminating, and explaining the Word of God like precious few of his national and international peers.*"
—**Author M. Rutledge McCall,** former Managing Senior Editor, Whitaker House Publishing; Developmental Editor of nearly three dozen books by noted theologians, pastors and Christian university professors worldwide

# Knowing God's Voice

"Ken Ulmer is one of America's new voices, rising with a penetrating call to pragmatic spiritual dynamics. As a Christian leader, he stands tall; as a servant to society, he stands out; as a friend, he stands trustworthy; as a man of God, he stands close--in touch with our Father, that he might be in touch with Him whose touch can change the world. Knowing Dr. Ulmer as I do, I attest to this: the man is real to the core! The truths with which he inspires multitudes becomes real and livable because he is relating what he's learned and lived and proven."

—**Jack W. Hayford**, President, Foursquare Churches International; Chancellor, The King's College and Seminary; Founding Pastor, The Church On The Way

"Bishop Kenneth Ulmer reveals from Scripture just how completely and fantastically our great God and Savior loves and cares for us, illuminating facets of His being that many believers have no doubt never considered."

—**Dr. Bill Bright,** Founder of Campus Crusade for Christ

"Dr. Ulmer is one of the most strategic Christian leaders in the nation. His impact in helping people understand God's principles for life is enriching while remaining biblical. It is hard to overstate the impact Dr. Ulmer makes on tens of thousands of Christians every week. This is a man who is truly on fire for Christ and longing to help others grow in Him."

—**Dr. Mark Brewer,** author, former Senior Pastor, Bel Air Presbyterian Church; Los Angeles, California

*"Dr. Ken Ulmer does what he does best. He slices through the confusion, misunderstanding and misinformation and then clearly and accurately explains the Scripture."*
—**Robert Morris,** Best-selling author; Lead Senior Pastor, Gateway Church

## Making Your Money Count

*"In Making Your Money Count, Dr. Kenneth Ulmer clearly articulates biblically-sound truth on the topic of money. I'm amazed at how often the subject of money is misinterpreted and distorted, but Dr. Ulmer brings us back to what the Bible really has to say on money and how we should use what we have. Dr. Ulmer is a great teacher, preacher, man of God and personal friend. Pick up this book, and prepare to be changed!"*
—**John Bevere,** Author and Speaker, Co-founder, Messenger International, Colorado Springs, Australia, United Kingdom

*"I would urge anyone who wants to know God's process for lifting people from poverty to financial productivity and wise money management to read this book! If you deal with money--whether you are rich, poor or in between--this book is for you. If you want to learn how to ease your monetary struggles...and help others who may be struggling financially, this book shows you how. It contains new thinking on a psychological and biblical foundation that I applaud."*
—**Dr. Robert H. Schuller;** Crystal Cathedral, California

*"The kingdom of God wants the God of the kingdom to invade every aspect of your world. In Making Your Money Count, Dr. Kenneth C. Ulmer will both instruct and illustrate for you how to turn your financial dreams into your fulfilled destiny. When you finish this book, you will view your wealth from God's perspective, and prosperity will have a life-changing purpose."*
—**Rev. Sunday Adelaja,** Senior Pastor and Founder, Embassy of God; Kiev, Ukraine

*"Making Your Money Count is about godliness, obedience, trust, maturity and biblical wisdom. Dr. Kenneth C. Ulmer has gathered scriptural evidence and exegeted the text as well as the context. In this book, he will lead you to a comprehensive understanding of how God views all things you. Read and grow into all that God purposes for you."*
—**Dr. Samuel R. Chand,** Leadership Development Consultant

*"The greatest law in God's universe is sowing and reaping, especially in the area of money. In Making Your Money Count, Dr. Kenneth C. Ulmer clearly teaches us how to move from spending to investing and from seeing what money can do to what money represents in our lives. If you truly want to achieve God's destiny in the years ahead, this invaluable resource is a must-read."*
—**Dr. James O. Davis,** Co-founder, Global Pastors Network; Billion Soul Initiative Ambassador, Orlando, Florida

*"Ken Ulmer is a trusted friend, and Making Your Money Count is a written testimony of his life and practice. As one who deeply loves and serves the Lord, Ken writes with authority and passion. You will be encouraged, challenged and blessed as you apply the simple, yet often misunderstood and neglected teachings presented in this book."*
—**Max Ellzey,** Chairman, The C12 Group; Los Angeles, California

*"Don't make the mistake of thinking that this book is going to be preachy and impractical! Kenneth Ulmer is keenly aware of what it takes to make your money count. Make friends with this book if you want to manage your resources successfully."*
—**Teresa Hairston,** Publisher and CEO, *Gospel Today* magazine

*"In Making Your Money Count, we're given a solid resource from a leader who provides us with the whole package: a book written by a wise pastor, a balanced teacher, a thorough-going scholar, a Bible-preacher and a passionate and godly man. It's a special delight to commend this evenhanded, insightful and practical tool that untwists a subject chat's too often mangled by poor exposition or distorted by exaggeration. You have to be happy when stewarding our finances is made alive and done right!"*
—**Jack W Hayford,** President, Foursquare Churches International; Chancellor, The King's College and Seminary; Founding Pastor, The Church On The Way

*"Making Your Money Count is a rhema word for the Body of Christ. Bishop Kenneth Ulmer counters the critic's question of whether God wants us to be rich with solid fundamental truths found throughout the Bible. This book is astounding and is certain to teach and empower God's children and critics as well."*
—**Bishop Eddie L. Long,** New Birth Baptist Church; Atlanta, Georgia

*"In Making Your Money Count, Dr. Ken Ulmer does what he does best. He slices through the confusion, misunderstanding and misinformation and then clearly and accurately explains the Scripture. Satan does not want you to read this book because hell will be plundered, heaven will be populated, and you will be blessed and be a blessing!"*
—**Robert Morris,** Senior Pastor, Gateway Church; Best-selling author, *The Blessed Life*

"*Bishop Kenneth Ulmer is one of the truly great spiritual leaders of our time. In this powerful and penetrating book, Bishop Ulmer plumbs the depths of the biblical meaning of prosperity. He confronts the false teaching of both the divine right presumption and the anti-prosperity predispositions in contemporary Christianity. Here is a benchmark book by a dynamic scholar preacher that is inspiring and instructive.*"
—**Dr. Lloyd John Ogilvie,** Former Chaplain, United States Senate

"*A false balance is an abomination to the LORD, but a just weight is His delight" (Proverbs 11:1). In the Scriptures, there are only 500 verses on prayer but more than 2,000 on abundance, money and prosperity. In Making Your Money Count, Dr. Ulmer masterfully unravels the divine path to wealth from God's perspective. This is a must-read for all those who are serious in honoring God with their wealth.*"
—**Dr. Robb Thompson,** President and CEO, Excellent Funding

"*It is said that among all the parables in the Bible, two-thirds of them speak to the issue of money. We all grapple with the question of how to be good stewards of our resources. What a blessing it is that Bishop Kenneth Ulmer has written a practical guide on the subject based on God's Word. Thank you, Bishop!*"
—Actors **Angela Bassett** and **Courtney B. Vance**

## The Champion in You

"*In a world that is filled with so many people who feel defeated or fearful, this word comes at a needy time. Bishop Kenneth Ulmer shares insights that transform the reader from the dismal to the dynamic. Take a read and watch the truths transform you until you emerge undaunted a champion for Christ!*"
—**Bishop T.D. Jakes, Sr.;** Potter's House of Dallas

"This book will unlock what God has destined each of us to be, and that is, a champion. This isn't some quick-fix, gimmick-filled book. Bishop Ulmer gives practical biblical principles that will inform you and help you to lead a transformed and empowered life. This book will change your life."

**—Bishop Noel Jones**

"Are you building your life for the eternal or the temporal? Are you striving to be an eternal champion, or one of this life only? God's ultimate desire is for you to be a champion in this life and eternity! But in order to do this, we must know what God has called us to, and we must each day choose to follow the path that God has laid out before us. My prayer is that as you read this book God would stir in your heart to be a champion in your generation."

**—John Bevere,** Author, Speaker, Messenger International, Colorado Springs, Australia, United Kingdom

"This is a very exciting book! It is a can't-put-it-down page-turner by one of today's most inspiring communicators. In The Champion In You, Kenneth Ulmer vividly portrays a divinely inspired, powerful biblical truth: God has placed within each of us a champion waiting to be discovered and released to be used for His glory and the encouragement of all those around us. If you want to get acquainted with this champion in you, this book will show you the way!"

**—Dr. Lloyd John Ogilvie,** Former Chaplain, United States Senate

## The Power of Money: How to Avoid A Devil's Snare

*"Such a balanced Biblical teaching! This is a topic that too many preachers today teach as a 'name it and claim it and blab it and grab it' theology. Bishop Ulmer has great wisdom and insight on the subject of mammon."*
—**Pastor Benny Hinn** (as quoted on "This is Your Day")

## In His Image

*"My dear friend, Bishop Kenneth Ulmer, is one of the most outstanding, creative preachers of our time. With* In His Image, *he has given us creative biblical treasure that will not only capture our minds but will also move our hearts toward a God whose heart is moved toward us. Reading this book will compel you to love God more deeply and to worship Him more fully!"*
—**Dr. Crawford W. Loritts, Jr.,** Speaker, Author, Radio host, Associate Director, Campus Crusade for Christ

*"In* In His Image, *Bishop Kenneth Ulmer reveals from Scripture just how completely and fantastically our great God and Savior loves and cares for us, illuminating facets of His being that many believers have no doubt never considered."*
—**Dr. Bill Bright,** Founder of Campus Crusade for Christ

# DEDICATION

*This project is dedicated to the team of colleagues who helped in the collaboration of the various moving parts of such an effort:*

*To the apple of my eye, the beat of my heart, the wind beneath my wings of over 40 years, Lady Togetta Ulmer,*

*To my uniquely gifted writing partner of many years, Michael McCall,*

*To my hi-tech "preaching partners," Derrick Pete and Tammy Harper,*

*To my beloved son, in whom I am well pleased, who travels the world with me and teaches me how to present much of this material with visuals and graphics, Kendan Christopher Ulmer,*

*To my friend, my sister in the Lord, and gifted transcriber, Robbin Hill,*

*To my faithful teaching assistant, Ashley King,*

*To the students of The King's University, who have taught me so much along my journey of healing, enlightenment, and grace, and*

*To my brother from another mother, who demonstrates that walls can fall, Dr. Robert Morris.*

# TABLE OF CONTENTS

# INTRODUCTION

The issue of race in America has always been, and continues to be, a contentious and thorny issue. Over the last two years, however, it has become even more divisive and cantankerous than ever. Then-candidate Donald Trump's barefaced demand for President Obama to prove his American pedigree by producing his birth certificate stuck like a hammer blow to the heads of millions of blacks, who have only relatively recently been given the rights of suffrage.

America's 2016 Presidential election was most certainly a watershed event in the history of American evangelicalism. While blacks in America, and particularly the black church, have been torn between the progressive social policies of the Democratic Party on the one hand and the religious, moral and ethical conservatism of the Republican Party on the other, the election in 2016 for many was a point of departure for blacks who, broadly speaking, would classify themselves within the evangelical camp. During this election cycle, pundits and pollsters discussed the "evangelical" vote and whether Republican candidate—a twice-divorced casino owner who swore with ease—would hold onto these stalwart supporters of the GOP.

Surprisingly for many, exit polls showed white evangelical voters voted in high numbers for Donald Trump, at 80%, and 16% for Hillary Clinton. The high numbers of white evangelicals who voted for a candidate whom many blacks considered a "racist" and many in the black church considered morally unfit to lead, widened the racial chasm within evangelicalism.

Many blacks who care to carry the badge "evangelical" and have struggled to find a place within the broader white evangelicalism movement have carved out a niche within the field of reconciliation. This noble task of reconciliation, loosely linked to the Civil Rights movement, was crystallized in the work of the *National Black Evangelical Association*, which defines itself as "An African American focused Ministry of Reconciliation" since 1963, and has as its motto, "Unity in Diversity Without Enforced Conformity," is championed by such black leaders as, Tom Skinner, William Bentley, Ruth Bentley, William Pannell, John Perkins, Walter McCray and the author of this book, Bishop Kenneth Ulmer, to name but a few.

Yet, unfortunately, the call for racial reconciliation has yielded little fruit over the years, and even with the historic triumph of a black man as President, America remains as divided as ever. The frustration with what the apostle Paul terms as "the ministry of reconciliation" has been tangibly expressed through texts such as *Reconciliation Blues* by Edward Gilbreath and *My Friend the Enemy* by William Pannell.

In *Walls Can Fall*, Bishop Ulmer urges the church to struggle on with the task of racial reconciliation in spite of its battle-worn scars. The book, which was developed from an extended sermon series under the book's title, struck a chord with the weekly adherents who attend the Faithful Central Bible Church or tune in online. The book takes a practical and graspable hands-on and heartfelt approach to living out racial reconciliation.

*Walls Can Fall* seeks to speak into the racial fatigue that blacks are feeling and the seeming lack of progress with race relations in spite of eight years of a black presidency and multiple book volumes, talks, films, etc., addressing the issue of Race in America. Ongoing police killings of unarmed black people, racial insults raining down from the Executive Branch of the government, gentrification, redlining, voter suppression, and the ongoing trauma of being black in America, in the words of Marvin Gay, "Makes me wanna holla." Sensing the weariness within his community and around the country regarding the slow pace of change toward our arrival at racial sobriety, Bishop Ulmer urges us to return to the

Holy Book for answers. Taking a practical, biblical and theological approach, injected with humor and personal anecdotes, the book brings into plain view God's big picture for humanity where there is "neither Jew nor Gentile, neither slave nor free, nor is there male and female, for you are all one in Christ Jesus."

—**Dr. Clifton Clarke,** Professor,
Fuller Theological Seminary;
Pasadena, California

# 1

# THE GRACE OF RACE

*1968 was shaping up to be one very memorable year.*

*Our frat was throwing a party when I heard about the shooting over WLAC, a 50,000-watt radio station from Nashville, which programmed R&B music at night to over half of America with DJs who were white but sounded just like black men. We students would argue over whether the jocks on Randy's (the nickname of the station, after its main sponsor, Randy's Records) were white guys skilled and talented to talk and sound black, or if they actually were black. I don't recall if it was Hoss Man or John R who was on the air that night, breaking the sad news, but WLAC was the voice that spoke to the handful of black students all the way from Nashville.*

*With the blanket of gloom hanging over campus in the wake of the cowardly gun-down of Dr. Martin Luther King, Jr., in the Memphis hotel where he had been staying, we students—members of Alpha Phi Alpha Fraternity at the University of Illinois—wanted to get the heaviness out of our systems and our minds off the incessant slaughter raging across the nation. But we weren't sure if a party was the right thing to do or the wrong thing to do.*

*It would turn out to be both.*

\* \* \*

I am a recovering racist. By the grace of God and by the power of the Holy Spirit, after seven decades on planet Earth, I am, in the present continual tense, being healed daily by the power of God.

Some of us are familiar with how 12-step programs work. A new member of the group will stand and say something like, "Hi.

My name of John. I'm an alcoholic." You don't get to attach titles or accolades or letters to your introduction. You're *John*, period. Not Dr. John, not Professor John, not John, Ph.D. It's not about puffing you up; it's not about rank, anonymous honesty. The others in the group will respond with a sincere and empathetic, "Hi, John." John might then go on to say something along the lines of, "I've been clean and sober for 35 years. But I'm an alcoholic—meaning I'm still in the recovery process, even after 35 years, still being healed."

If I were in RA (Raceaholics Anonymous—There's no such organization but there should be.), I'd have to introduce myself with something like, "Hi. My name is Ken. I'm a raceaholic."

I'm not in a 12-step program, but I'm still a recovering racist. I trust God every day of my life to heal me of race-related scars and wounds that are decades old. I find myself struggling with my deliverance as I see or hear the observations and declarations of political, sociological, and ecclesiastical pundits on the topic of racism in America.

Recent polls have confirmed that Americans are bitterly split on the topic of racism. A Gallup poll conducted just after America's 2016 presidential election found 77 percent of Americans see the country as "greatly divided when it comes to the most important values,"[1] an increase from 66 percent in 2012. A Washington Post-University of Maryland poll conducted nine months into Trump's presidency found that seven in 10 Americans thought the nation's political divisions were as bad as during the Vietnam War.[2] Historians are also raising the alarm over a spike in division across America. In early March of 2019, historian and author Livia Gershon revealed things had deteriorated even further since a poll taken in the wake of the Trump inauguration in 2017.[3]

---

1   See: http://news.gallup.com/poll/197828/record-high-americans-perceive-nation-divided.aspx
2   See: https://www.washingtonpost.com/classic-apps/its-just-messed-up-most-think-political-divisions-as-bad-as-vietnam-era-new-poll-shows/2017/10/27/e359d5b8-bb53-11e7-be94-fabb0f1e9ffb_story.html
3   Livia Gershon, "Five historians dissect the country's divisions in the era of Donald

The rise of widespread use of social media, combined with the decline of the central institutions that once defined the borders of political debate, have created a potentially dangerous moment in our public discourse. Even disasters seem to pull us more apart rather than bring us together. In the wake of mass shootings in Sutherland Springs, Texas, and Las Vegas, Nevada, and the devastation of Hurricane Maria in Puerto Rico, social media launched into full-throated partisan debate over how to view such events in the era of Donald Trump.[4]

On the issue of racial division in America, a Pew poll conducted in 2016 showed that 88 percent of blacks think more needs to be done to give blacks equal rights, while only 53 percent of whites thought so.[5] A CBS News-New York Times survey done the same year revealed that three-quarters of African Americans agreed that police are more likely to use deadly force against a black person than a white person; whereas, only half of white Americans agreed.[6]

Lest we drown in the depressing dilemma of the troubled waters of our cultural climate and feel locked in a chokehold of powerlessness, let's zoom out the lens and look at one other perspective from a Pew Research Center article in the spring of 2019 that might be helpful in reflecting on my personal "race rehab" struggle:

"More than 150 years after the 13th Amendment abolished slavery in the United States, most U.S. adults say the legacy of slavery continues to have an impact on the position of black people in American society today. More than four-in-ten say the country hasn't made enough progress toward racial equality, and there is some skepticism, particularly among blacks, that black people will ever have equal rights with whites...."[7]

---

Trump." See: https://www.history.com/author/livia-gershon

4   Ibid

5   See: http://www.pewsocialtrends.org/2016/06/27/on-views-of-race-and-inequality-blacks-and-whites-are-worlds-apart/

6   The *Washington Post*: "America really is more divided than ever", By Joel Achenbach and Scott Clement; July 16, 2016. Also see: http://www.nytimes.com/2016/07/14/us/most-americans-hold-grim-view-of-race-relations-poll-finds.html

7   Pew Research Center, April 9, 2019; "Race in America 2: Public has negative views of the country's racial progress; more than half say Trump has made race relations worse"; by Juliana Menasce Horowitz, Anna Brown and Kiana Cox. See: https://www.pewresearch.

Long before I was intellectually capable of dissecting or even discerning the nuances and dangers of such an openly fragmented society, I experienced a life-shaping trauma in a microcosm of reality half a century ago that still exists to this day.

When I was around 10 years old, I was the only black student taking piano lessons at a school in East St. Louis, Illinois, called the Shield's School of Music. All of the students were being taken on a fieldtrip to an amusement event. The venue was a huge steamship called the *Admiral*, which is docked at the foot of the harbor on the St. Louis side of the Mississippi River. People would board the Admiral and sail up and down the Mississippi River for a few hours of fun, fellowship, and entertainment provided by a Lawrence Welk-type band (an all-white orchestra) that played dance music such as the fox-trot, the waltz, and other ballroom songs.

On this particular Saturday, we students of the Shield's School of Music were being taken on this fieldtrip no doubt to expose us to the musical styles of the big band sound. I wore my Sunday suit and Sunday shoes on the outing.[8] My daddy was on my left side, holding my left hand, and my mother was holding my right hand as we were coming down a ramp to where the big ship was docked.

At the bottom of the ramp were two white men, one of whom was dressed in all white, and, as I recall, the other one was wearing a Smokey the Bear-type hat. Smokey was some kind of a local police force. He was standing there all official looking, with his muscle-bound arms folded across his chest, examining everyone as they proceeded on their way to board the Admiral like they were entering a prison yard.

When my parents and I got to the end of the dock, Smokey Bear growled, "Where you all going?"

"Why, we're going on The Admiral," my mama said with a smile.

---

org/staff/juliana-menasce-horowitz, https://www.pewresearch.org/staff/anna-brown and https://www.pewresearch.org/staff/kiana-cox

8   Some readers may recall days when we didn't have a wardrobe; we had our Sunday shoes and Sunday suit, which we didn't wear to play in or go to school in. It was Sunday clothes and everything else.

"Not today, you ain't," he barked.

"You don't understand," she smiled again. "See, the Shield's School is going on the Admiral, and my son here is a student at the school."

"We don't allow Niggas on this here boat."

The sudden quiet and steely gaze in his eyes told us he was boss, and we were Niggas, and that's all there was to discuss.

Mama said sweetly, so as not to rile the bear, "Sir, we're with the school of music, and my son is going with the whole school," pointing to the other kids, both ahead and behind us, "See? That's them, there."

"I don't care who's going. We don't allow Niggas on this boat, and if y'all don't get away from here," (He jabbed his finger in my dad's face and looked him hard in the eyes.) "we're gunna run you in." *Deal with you uppity Niggas. Put you in yo place. Lock you up for, for—heck, just* bein' *here.*

I looked up, trying to make contact with my daddy's eyes as he stared silently into the white cop's ample face. All the while, the cop kept his finger in my daddy's face as they stood there, eyeball to eyeball, man to man. Master to slave. All over again. A hundred years after the Civil War was to have settled such crass issues.

Seven decades later, I still remember that scene as clearly as if it took place yesterday. A black man does not forget such encounters. And that one was downright civil compared to other experiences I've had.

As I write this, I am 71 years old (I don't look it, don't act it, but too often can't help but feel it!), and I forever have the look on my daddy's face seared into my memory like a cattle brand from the day when a white man spoke to him like he was an errant little boy, in front of his own son. I've never forgotten it. I can't forget it. Won't forget it. It's part of who a particular segment of American society insists I am to this day. Nothing but a nigger, to them.

A few years ago, when I was about 68, I was a speaker at the E. K. Bailey Conference on Expository Preaching at the Fairmont Hotel in Dallas, Texas. A driver was assigned to pick me up at the airport and drop me off at the hotel. He picked me up in a big, shiny black SUV. We arrived at the Fairmont, and I got out and stretched, waiting for the bellman to grab my bags, when a white lady pulled in behind our SUV, got out, held her keys to me without even looking at me, and said, "Take care of my car, boy."

I was heading toward 70 years old at the time, and I wasn't going to be any *boy*. And I *definitely* wasn't that southern woman's antediluvian idea of a boy. So, that was her first problem. Her second problem was that I'm from East St. Louis. And, as I mentioned, I'm a recovering racist. It didn't take but a nanosecond to crash my mind back to the south end of East St. Louis. Fortunately, during that nanosecond, a news headline flashed across my mind too as I assessed how to respond to the lady. *Mega Church Pastor Decks White Female Guest at Prestigious Fairmont Hotel!*

Mustering all the calm I could, I said to her, "Ma'am. Do I look like I work here?"

That's the best line I could come up with in my state of shock and still remain spiritual while under racial attack.

Wasn't the first time such a thing had happened to me, either. A few years after that incident I was boarding a plane on my way to speak at a conference and had to change planes in Chicago. My host had paid for my travel and sent me a first-class ticket.

I was in the priority line, waiting to board, when an attendant said to me, "Sir, this is the first-class line."

Now, first of all, I can read pretty well. I have four earned degrees, including two doctorates, have delivered a few thousand sermons and written a dozen books, and so forth. I certainly could read *Priority, First-class, Economy* and so on. So, we launch into a vigorous discussion on the merits of my being in the wrong line.

She then looks at my boarding pass—*and calls over another agent* to chime in on the matter! True story. God bless her, maybe she couldn't read an airline ticket. Maybe she thought a 70-year-old man couldn't. Who knows?

Another true story. Several years before that I was on my way to Israel. I had spoken at a conference in the New York area, and my wife and I were to join a group led by one of my best long-time friends, Dr. Jack Hayford, to visit the Holy Land. We were preparing to go through security at JFK when we were pulled out of the line and taken to a side room.

I understand what security is all about. Especially in this post-9-11 world. So, my wife and I were taken into separate rooms for awhile, then we were brought back together for further inquiries, so they could see if our stories matched or diverged. Because there's only *one reason* a person is invited for a private chat in The Room at an airport.

In my room, I was asked the standard questions. *What is the purpose of your travel? How long will you be in Israel? Where will you be staying?* I get all that. Makes sense. But then they asked me some questions that were a little, shall we say, *offbeat*:

"Do you always travel business?"

"Not always. Depends."

"How can you afford to fly business?"

"What?"

"Who paid for your ticket?"

"The church. Why are you ask—"

"How can a church afford to pay for a business-class ticket?"

And so forth. For over an hour. After which they finally let us go.

I felt embarrassed as I held my wife's shivering hand, and we made our way to boarding. I felt like a criminal. Like I was flashed back to the line as a little kid at the Admiral under the gaze of Smokey the cop. I felt helpless—I *was* helpless. Worthless. Little.

Insignificant. And *deeply* wounded that we would be treated this way in the new millennium in the nation of our birth.

But, there was nothing I could do about it.

So, I happen to be a recovering racist. And I declare unto you that the God who is a healer can heal racial wounds. I declare unto you that racism is a sin out of the arsenal of the demonic. I declare unto you that it is but by the grace of God and the power of the Spirit of God that healing can come forth, even from racial wounds, whether inflicted by fellow believers or unbelievers.

Maybe you too bear scars, bruises, and wounds of prejudices, biases, and curses that have been thrown into your life and passed down from one generation to the next. Maybe you are plagued by visions and images and pictures in your minds of how your parents and grandparents and uncles and aunts and generations gone before have been treated or treated others. What's the answer now, in this generation and moving forward? Do any models exist to help us understand and deal with the insidious roots of racism and ethnic discrimination? Yes—several, including Luke and Paul.

Dr. Luke wrote two books in the canon of Scripture. He wrote the Gospel of Luke and the book of Acts (which opens with a link and a connection to the Gospel of Luke). I call Luke the original civil rights advocate, freedom fighter, and model in the battle for racial equality. Of the four writers of the Gospels, Luke is the premiere one who, in and through his writings, advocates and highlights more than any other writer the unity across racial lines that is in the very heart of our living God. In any discourse on the importance of identifying, understanding and eradicating any thread of racism within us, it is important to learn from the consistency of Luke's writings the revelation of a theology that can bring forth healing—even in this astonishingly troubled, messed-up, jacked-up world in which we live.

From the very beginning, it was God's will that the earth be filled with His glory (Psalm 72:19). How does He do that? He fills the earth with His glory through His people. The people of God includes all the people from the generations of Adam and Eve. Thus, it was God's plan from the generations of Adam and Eve that the earth be filled with His glory and that such glory would come by all the races included in the earth realm.

Apostle Paul picks up that vision and looks way down the road to give us a hint to the key of the theology of Luke, which is the connection to the blessing of Abraham. Everything that follows revolves around this connection revelation.

In Galatians 3:7, Paul echoes Lucan theology when he says those who have faith—that is, believers—are the children of Abraham. That's the key. We are children of Abraham. In Galatians 3:8, Paul explains that "Scripture foresaw that God would justify the Gentiles...." A Gentile is everybody who is not a Jew. In other words, *all* the other races, *all* the other beliefs, *all* the other people who come forth who are not Jewish are included in the term "Gentile." Continuing with Paul's explanation so "that God would justify the Gentiles by faith and announced the gospel in advance to Abraham."

So, God announced the gospel to Abraham first, before anyone else. This means that the Gospel of God, the Gospel of Christ, the Gospel of the Kingdom, was revealed first in the life of Abraham for the benefit of his Gentile seed, the children of Abraham. Here's why; continuing the verse: so that "All nations will be blessed through you." Those first two words contain the key: *all* nations. The word for "nations" is the word *ethnos*, from which we get our word *ethnicity*. In other words, *all ethnicities will be blessed through Abraham*. Not only Semitic, Jewish, Caucasian, African, Asian, Eskimo or whatever—but ALL nations.

Now on to verses 9 and 14, continuing with Paul's explanation of God's promise of salvation blessing: "So those who rely on faith are blessed along with Abraham, the man of faith" because God "redeemed us in order that the blessing given to Abraham might come to the Gentiles through Christ Jesus, so that by faith we might receive the promise of the Spirit."

So, we have Abraham. We have the blessing of Abraham. And we have the promise of the Spirit.

Now to verses 16 and 18, nailing it all down: "These promises were spoken to Abraham and to his seed [that's the Gentiles]— Scripture does not say 'and to seeds,' meaning many people, but 'and to your seed,' meaning one person, who is Christ." In other words, we are a seed of Abraham, and we are also the seed of Christ. Verse 18 continues, "For if the inheritance depends on the law, then it no longer depends on the promise; but God in His grace gave it to Abraham through a promise."

The reason this chapter is titled *The Grace of Race* is because God released grace to and through the races, the divergent ethnicities, that flowed from Abraham. God made a promise to Abraham, beginning in chapter 12 of the Book of Genesis, culminating from everything that happened between Genesis 3 to Genesis 12.

As a quick summary: the sin of Adam and Eve that changed the whole dynamic of the creation of God continues through to Genesis 10. After the global devastation of the flood, God started all over again. Yet, because of the sin of man, mankind became scattered and decided to build itself a tower to the heavens. Man had decided he wanted to be his own god and to create God in his own image (seemingly forgetting the very God who created him in the first place—something he could never do). In response to that, God allowed the sin that was already in men to confuse their unity, because man become arrogant enough to try to become his own god.

So, God scattered them, and, due to their inability to communicate with people outside of their own families or groups, they broke down into ethnicities (or "races"), and they dispersed throughout the earth.

The promise of God's Genesis 26 future blessings of Abraham begins back in Genesis 12, where God said, "I will bless you, Abraham. I will bless those who bless you. I will curse those who curse you. I will bless the nations through you." This Genesis 12 promise is restated in Genesis 26:4 as, "I will make your descendants [meaning Abraham] as numerous as the stars in the sky, and will give them all of these lands, the lands of the earth, and through your offspring all nations on earth will be blessed." So, there it is again: through Abraham, all nations ("nations" is the same word in Genesis and in Galatians—the word *ethnos*[9]), all ethnicities, throughout the world will be blessed through the promise and the blessing of Abraham.

That's the setup; the foundation of one race, one world, all nations, all equal, comes directly from the Word of God.

This banner for the equality of all people in the Kingdom of God and under His power is advocated most of all through the writings of Luke. (One could say that Dr. Disciple Luke was the Dr. Martin Luther King, Jr., of his day.) Luke begins his story by connecting the believers in Christ to a man named Abraham, where in Luke 1:54-55 he states that God "has helped His servant Israel, remembering to be merciful to Abraham and to the descendants of Abraham forever...." This applies to Abraham and the descendants of Abraham, the heirs of Abraham, the seed of Abraham, the children of Abraham, as he promised our ancestors.

So, in Luke chapter one, he takes the story, the birth and the coming of Christ, and emphasizes the universal dynamic of the scope of grace of the gospel of Christ, which is beyond and transcends all races or ethnicities. So, there it is again, nailing home from the beginning of Old Testament Scripture in Genesis that we are one race, one world, all nations, all equal. And if God

---

9   Regarding the word "nations" the LXX (The Greek Old Testament) generally translates gôy as éthnos, especially when the nations, excluding Israel, are in view (from *International Standard Bible Encyclopedia*, revised edition, ©1979 by Wm. B. Eerdmans Publishing Co. All rights reserved.)

Himself decreed it that way, who has the right to change what God has ordained?

Let's move on to Luke 2:30-32, where the good doctor makes a connection to the Abrahamic prophecy: Simeon, the righteous and devout man of God, takes the infant Jesus in His arms at the temple and praises God, saying, "For my eyes have seen your salvation, the salvation which you prepared in the sight of all nations [there's that phrase *all nations* again] a light for revelation to the Gentiles and the glory of your people Israel." What God is saying here is that there is a universal, international, transnational, trans-ethnic all-encompassing dynamic to the Kingdom of God. *Everyone*—in one basket. So, Luke opens his gospel by relating it all back to Abraham. Then, at the end, in Luke 24:47, he closes his gospel with the same emphasis: "And repentance for the forgiveness of sins will be preached in His name to all nations beginning at Jerusalem."

Now we fast-forward, because Luke has set the stage for part two of his writing, which I suggest is the Book of Acts. In Acts 1, verse 8 he says, "But you will receive power when the Holy Spirit comes on you." I like how the King James version states it: you shall receive power *after the Holy Ghost is come upon you*. Now finishing the verse: "and you shall be witnesses in Jerusalem, in all Judea and Samaria and to the ends of the earth." One version says, "to the uttermost parts of the world."

This witnessing shall be done not just to the Israelites, not only to the Babylonians, not merely to the Persians, the Greeks, Egyptians, Spaniards, Turks, Samarians. We're not limited to witnessing only to our fellow Africans, our fellow Western Europeans, fellow Mexicans, Central Americans, Eskimos, Chinese, Blacks, Whites, Browns and on and on, but to the ends of the earth, the uttermost parts of the world, to *everyone*. God does not delineate, segregate, eliminate, expurgate whom we are to tell of His greatness, love, and wonders.

In this passage, Jesus is on His way back to the Father, and before He ascends, He gives the commission and the authority to the disciples when He says, "You shall receive power." He is speaking about that power in John's writing in chapters 14, 15, and 16 when Jesus tells the disciples that when He goes to the Father, the Father will send another Comforter, Counselor, Holy Spirit, just like He is, and just as when He was with them, He will now be in them. And "When I go," God says, through Jesus, "you shall receive power."

Jesus said it would be through the power of the Holy Spirit that believers will be witnesses unto (*of, about, for*) Him. Your life as a believer will witness to and point to Him before *all* others—everyone you come into contact with. Our relationships with God are not to be undercover. You are not a secret-service saint. You are not to live incognito. You are not to avoid many and touch few. The Bible says *your life is to be a witness*. In fact, the structure of that sentence, you shall be witnesses in Jerusalem and to the ends of the earth, indicates it is not a suggestion. You are already a witness, so that's not the question; the question is this: *what kind of witness are you?* Because your life is a testimony every second that you are in eyesight or earshot of another human being—online, offline, phone line, doesn't matter. We are living, walking, breathing, 24/7/365 examples of what we think of our living, loving God, Creator of the entire universe and all that is in it. That means to *everyone*. In other words, our lives are really meant to be the witness of a powerful résumé and potent testimonial declaration of the power of the Spirit of God.

"You shall receive power after the Holy Ghost comes upon you." That's where it starts. And because of that power, you shall be witnesses. Where? In this passage, it's in Jerusalem, Judea, Samaria and the innermost parts of the world. In your passages in life, it's wherever you find yourself.

Moving on with the story, now to chapter two of Acts. Just

as Luke began the Book of Luke, he begins the Book of Acts in the same way. To summarize it, the disciples and apostles are all together, the place is filled with the sound of a rushing, mighty wind, and they all begin to speak in tongues. The tongues issue is significant, because it speaks of *languages*—the very ability that was once used to the point of abuse when mankind was all one and all spoke one language and which God disrupted because the people were using language to try to engineer an anointment and appointment of themselves as god.

Fast forward thousands of years later, and our patient God is still moving things forward unrestricted by the concept of time, still working His plan to get mankind to choose to all be on the same page per His grand design and desire for the unity of humanity under His loving grace and care.

Luke lets us know that what began in that little room could not be contained within that room. This means that what God is doing in your life can never be contained in just your life. It has to go outward from you. What God is doing in your home can never be contained in just your home. What God is doing in your life must spill out into the revelation of what the world sees, because what people see in you should reflect the God who is in you, the same God who is no respecter of persons—meaning, He does not hold one person or group of people in higher esteem than others. He's an equal opportunity lover. Loves us all the same.

Moving on to the next verse, Acts 2:5, we get a roll call of who's in the scene: "Now, there were staying [residing] in Jerusalem God-fearing Jews from every nation under heaven." There's our phrase again: *every nation under heaven*. This means that by the time they got to Pentecost, there were representatives from all over the then-known world, gathered as nations, as *ethnos*, ethnicities. There are representatives from all ethnicities over the world that was known at the time. And they were bewildered as to what was going on.

Acts 2:6-8: "When they heard this sound, a crowd came together in bewilderment, because each one heard their own language being spoken. Utterly amazed, they asked, 'Aren't all of these who are speaking Galileans? How is it then that each of us hears in our own native language?'" Now comes the roll call of who's present; verse 9: "Parthians, Medes and Elamites; residents of Mesopotamia, Judea, Cappadocia, Pontus and Asia." Stop there for a moment of reflection: there were Asians there. Isn't it interesting that most discussions today about racism relate almost strictly to white and black, and seldom, if ever, do we acknowledge or even realize that there is similar bias, prejudice and racism, between whites and Asians and blacks and Asians and Hispanics and so forth? We humans have devolved into equal opportunity racists.

Here's what we need to see in this example from Acts 2: on the day they were all together in the room, *Asians were among them!* In many places in the world today, there are just as much schism and division and suspicion and animosity against Asians as there are against blacks. Yet, it's important to understand that Asians were in the group at Pentecost.

People in the Hispanic nations and countries might well ask why Hispanics weren't specifically mentioned in this group. The purpose of the "roll call" of the group may not have been intended to be an exhaustive, all-inclusive list of the different ethnicities, but there is a hint about Hispanics, in Luke 6:13-16, where we read that two of the 12 disciples were named *James*. One was James, the brother (more precisely, half-brother) of Jesus. The other James was a sort of cousin of Jesus and son of a man named Alphaeus. This James, son of Alphaeus, was often called James the Lesser. James the brother of Jesus became the pastor of the first church and was later killed and beheaded. And here's what one church history tradition suggests happened to James the Lesser:

"What may actually have happened was that the apostle St.

James was ordered to preach Christianity in Hispania after the death of Jesus Christ, sometime around the year 40 AD. The apostle arrived at a southern port on the Iberian peninsula, making use of the busy Roman maritime traffic. He went north through Portugal and arrived at Iria Flavia, where he continued to preach and to move eastwards. Around two years after his arrival, He decided to return to Palestine. When he got back to his homeland, he was denounced by the Jews, and Herod Agrippa ordered him to be decapitated. His disciples brought his body to Spain for burial."[10]

This James the Lesser, tradition has it, took the gospel to Spain, in an area called Iberia, bringing the Latino, Hispanic, Spanish-speaking nations into the gospel of Christ. (I find it interesting that sometimes even in my city, Los Angeles, the stories that fill the headlines are more often about the tension over gang turf and warfare between black gangs and Hispanic gangs.)

Now, back to Pentecost as Acts 2:9 continues with the list of those present: "Phrygia and Pamphylia, Egypt and the parts of Libya near Cyrene, visitors from Rome (both Jews and converts to Judaism); Cretans and Arabs...." All the nations were there. Notice that there were nations from northern Africa there, too.

I was 30 years old before I discovered there were black people in the Bible. I used to think everybody in the Bible, including Jesus, was white. I was amazed there were people from Africa in the Bible. But in fact, not only were blacks at Pentecost, there were blacks who were leaders in the church, including—brace yourself, now—*prophets and apostles*. In Acts 13:1, two men are identified as prophets and teachers, leaders in the Church. One was Simeon, who was called Niger. When I first read that, it kind of scared me. Niger? The Niger in *Africa*? Prophets and teachers? Then crystal clarity was added when I read it in other versions. *The Amplified Bible* calls Simeon "black." Wow. Talk about a bombshell of truth; and it was there all the time.

---

10   See: http://musmon.com/en/content/64/en/CatedralDeSantiagoDeCompostela/2

Now, I think I know what some readers are thinking. But c'mon, work with me here. You *know* that brother Lucius had to be of a chocolate hue. Lucius is a common African American name. In fact, one of the members of my leadership team is named Lucius. I may be saying that somewhat tongue in cheek, but I say it to make the point: *these first-century church leaders were black.* "Simeon, that was called Niger"—the name has the same root as the word *negro.* "Lucius" was of Cyrene—an African settlement. Simeon was black. He might have been an African; and Lucius was definitely African.[11] To deny that is to admit disinterest in Biblical fact.

As a student of Scripture with a passionate motivation for exegesis and biblical interpretation, I strain to make certain I present the text with relevance and accuracy, yet with a desire to bridge the gap between the times and cultures of the text and that in which we live today. And I find it interesting how many scholars and commentators find it insignificant that there were high-level people of color in the first church. Not people sitting in the balcony of marginalized observation, not slaves or beggars, but people of color *in critical positions of spiritual influence.* That is a significant fact in the world God created.

Abbott, Darby, G. Campbell Morgan, the *Geneva Bible*, Hawker's *Poor Man's Commentary*, and Holman's *Bible Handbook* (and I'm sure other noted liturgical, biblical research sources) make literally no mention of the ethnicity of two key leaders in the first church. As I studied these reference materials, I found it curiously obvious that they either completely miss or apparently see no importance in mentioning that there were men of color in the critical crossroads passage of Acts 13. It's a critical passage in that it set the stage for the next level of fulfillment of the missionary dynamic of the commission left by our Lord to *go into all the world and make disciples.*

I am, however, encouraged by the hermeneutic of such

---

11   *The Biblical Illustrator*, © 2002, 2003, 2006; Ages Software, Inc. and Biblesoft, Inc.

scholars as Harry Ironside in his prophetic kingdom observation of Acts 13:1-3:

"Then 'Simeon that was called Niger'—that is, 'Simeon the black man.' We wish we knew more about him. He is the one outstanding man in the New Testament who comes before us as a servant of God from the Negro race. There was no racial prejudice in this church. People of different color skin and of different religious background were found happily worshiping together-Jews, Gentiles, people of various races. This is all we read of Simeon, yet it is enough to tell us that the grace of God was working in a mighty way, breaking down carnal prejudice."[12]

Thus, careful investigative scrutiny of the text reveals that there are black people in the Bible. There are Asians in the Bible. (Peter writes his first letter and addresses it to believers who are in Asia.) The Bible include Hispanics. (In the closing chapters in his letter to the Romans, in Romans 15:28, Paul says, "I will go to Spain.") And on and on. The gospel would include *all races*. And this grace of race connects and traces back to a man named Abraham. Paul says in Galatians 3:16 that it was because of our relationship with God that the promise of blessing to Abraham and the seed that comes through him, the seed that Isaiah said is through the Messiah, the seed that comes through Jesus, the Christ. We discover that his "seed" includes all ethnicities, because through him, the Bible says, *all nations will be blessed*. And all means *all*.

The word *ethnic* (which gives us "ethnicity") is a comprehensive and multidimensional word that can mean at least four things. Ethnicity refers to your look, your likes; it refers to your language, your liturgy. "All ethnicities" means all of those in the various racial groupings. It means how a person appears physically and assumes we all look different from one another. The idea of ethnicity is acknowledgment of racial physical differences and

---

12   *Ironside Commentaries*, Acts 13:1-3; PC Study Bible formatted electronic database, © 2012 by Biblesoft, Inc. All rights reserved.

presupposes that by God's design there is variety in this creation of humanity. God says that because of His power and love, ethnic difference encompasses and embraces all those who are different into the oneness of the love, the power, and the grace of God. It's about acknowledgment and acceptance of physical differences between people, regardless of ethnicity.

Sometimes it refers to our likes, our cultural distinctions. Often the word "ethnic" refers to the various mores and customs of a given people, their diet, their dress, their ways. In Africa, for example, sometimes you can tell different African nations and tribes by their clothing, the garb, the dress they wear. They have different languages, different likes, different styles, different customs.

My wife and I went to Scotland not long ago, and learned that each of the clans and tribes has a different pattern in the cloth of its garments, which displays and affirms the differences between clans. One of my dearest friends, the late Dr. Lloyd Ogilvie, former Chaplain of the United States Senate, was proud of his Scottish ethnicity and often displayed it by the distinctive sartorial splendor of the green plaid kilt he wore that identified his family clan.

Sometimes cultural differences involve more than dress or cuisine or even skin color. Sometimes it's language differences. When the gospel went to Spain, the whole Spanish language, dialects and all, was brought into play. For example, Spanish and Portuguese are similar but different. There are Spanish idioms found in Spain that are different than in Mexico, and Central American phrases that are different than those in Cuba, though, they're all the same basic language. Likewise, there are cultural distinctions between a Latino from Mexico and a Latino from South America.

We're all different in many ways, but identical in one way: we're all God's creation. And He did a pretty colorful job in creating so many diverse human beings. Different is good, it's God, it's an attribute of the diversity in the unity of His creativity. But there are two extremes some people get trapped into. One is the concept of elevating certain differences and denigrating others. That creates *separation*. It's the devil who wants to twist *different* into *separate*.

The other extreme is colorblindness. I don't want to live in a colorblind society. I don't want you to be blind to my color, and I don't want to be blind to yours. My color is part of my identity. Don't just blindly look over me. Look at me and acknowledge our differences. (Maybe even celebrate them, as much as possible.) It's a trick of the enemy to convince us that justification of the invisibility of an ethnic or racial class is the same as accepting differences. It's not. Not having to acknowledge differences in others might allow us a certain level of personal comfort because we don't have to engage on a deeper level, and if you merely see me, you might be prone to paint me some color—and you've suddenly engaged in subtle separation.

Colorblindness is not God's goal. It's about seeing us all as children of God under the love of God, under the power of God, under the protection and covering of God. It's about us coming together across all the things that would separate us. It's about loving people beyond the external color and seeing their internal intrinsic value. A value given to each one of us by the God who wrapped that intrinsic value in a visible color, a unique hue, a compelling shade.

And sometimes ethnicity speaks of liturgy. This means that there are places where the Bible sees nations in terms of their religious distinctions. So, the term *nations*, in some places in the Bible, is talking about those who are idol worshipers. Those who worship Baal are those who are often spoken of as those who are from "the nations."

"Ethnicity" then, means your looks, your likes, customs, language, religion, and/or liturgy. The grace that is on race is based in the blessing of Abraham because, as Paul says, we are all heirs of Abraham; and as God said to Abraham, they will *all* be blessed.

We all have an inheritance, and it is for all who are in Christ and for all who are in the loving care and comfort of God. Yet, God never requires that we stop being the individuals we are, because we are who He made us. The catch is, He loves us the way He made us (Remember the old saying, *God doesn't make mistakes.*), and any desire to be something other than God has made you is a step in the direction of the temptation of bias and division and is not of God.

Let me be me. Let me see myself in the blessing of Abraham. Just as unique as you. Just as different as you. Just as human as you. Just as God-loved as you.

Prolific contemporary gospel artist Donald Lawrence picked up on this idea in his popular song, "The Blessing of Abraham."

> *It's Your Inheritance*
> *Get Your Inheritance*
> *You Are The Seed, By Faith Receive*
> *The Blessing Of Abraham*
> *The Blessing Of Abraham*[13]

## The Scars of Self-Image

Many people struggle with self-image. They struggle with who they see in the mirror, because of what society relegates us to, the boxes culture shoves us into. I believe much of the self-image problem today is related to our TGIF culture: Twitter, Google, Instagram, Facebook. (I learned this modern acronym from my friend and cultural prophet, Dr. Leonard Sweet.) Many of those wounds were passed down from one generation to the next. I'm not immune; I wear scars. I can't get out of my mind the look on my daddy's face when that white man talked to him at the *Admiral*, but I'm healed, and I'm being healed, by the power of the living God.

---

13   Lyrics by Donald Lawrence. Recorded by Donald Lawrence and the Tri-City Singers.

Luke says it's all connected to the power of the Holy Spirit. On the Day of Pentecost, it was in the presence of the Holy Spirit that the body (not "bodies") of Christ was formed. Here's a big statement that, in these present days fraught with ethnic separation, causes a disquieting clash within many self-admitted Christians and in many churches: *A spirit-filled church cannot tolerate or maintain a spirit of racism.* Because the filling of the Holy Spirit is what brought us Christians together in the first place. We cannot walk in the power of God or be filled with the Holy Spirit if we hate someone because of their chocolate-colored or vanilla-colored face. We cannot be filled with the love of God if we hate those who have a face or skin shade lighter or darker than ours. A spirit filled church can never maintain a spirit of hatred and prejudice and racism for any reason whatsoever. If it does, it is a house divided; its Kingdom testimony will not stand.

Trudging through the mine fields of this racial war zone in this new millennium requires that we delve into some very controversial topics. The core problem is that for too long, the church has stayed out of the discussion of race, prejudice, ethnic separation. And they have festered and increased and grown uglier by the year.

Part of the reason is because for the most part, the church has remained on the topic of racism mute, marginalized, and on the sidelines, with a deafeningly dead silence on the subject coming out of speakers from the microphones in pulpits across America— especially those of the Evangelical persuasion. Men and women who call themselves Christians, and particularly "Christian leaders," endanger the validity and credibility of their identity if they harbor a scintilla of deliberate separation or denigration of different cultures or ethnicities in their hearts or minds.

As we wrestle through this topic in light of racism against Asians and Hispanics, we will deal with questions raised by some black nationalists and some white supremacists: *How can a black man ever serve a white Jesus? How can a white man ever serve a black man?* At their core, these two questions are different sides of the same coin. So, let's tackle the first side. Was Jesus really *white?* If so, how did Jesus get white in the first place, when He was born in a Semitic culture? And does it really matter what color He was anyway?

In light of the discussions and debates over the issue of race, here's an interesting historical observation: in his June 22, 2018, article in the Brookings blog titled "US white population declines and Generation 'Z- Plus' is minority white, census shows,"[14] William H. Frey, author of *Diversity Explosion: How New Racial Demographics are Remaking America*, notes this:

"The U.S. Census Bureau's release of race and age statistics for 2017 points to two noteworthy milestones about the nation's increasingly aging white and growing diverse population. First, for the first time since the Census Bureau has released these annual statistics, they show an absolute decline in the nation's white non-Hispanic population—accelerating a phenomenon that was not projected to occur until the next decade."[15]

I understand that much of the reports of declining white population (particularly in counties such as Los Angeles, as well as in southwestern states such as Arizona, New Mexico, Texas and California) are disseminated and manipulated by right-winged fear-mongering supremacists. I raise the issue in the context of the discussion that the global growth of Christianity is facing a challenge posed in this question: *How do people of color serve and follow a "white Jesus?"*

Am I overreacting to a racial red herring? If we acknowledge

---

14   https://www.brookings.edu/book/diversity-explosion-2
15   https://www.brookings.edu/blog/the-avenue/2018/06/21/us-white-population-declines-and-generation-z-plus-is-minority-white-census-shows/

that God is "spirit," implying that He has no corporal observable color, then we must address the fact that our God chose to wrap Himself in flesh and blood and come into the world as a babe and as a male and with all the same limitations of humanity. Jesus who walked the earth had to look like *something*. He was seen for over three decades before He died and for forty days by hundreds after He rose from the tomb. He looked like something. He was recognized for more than 33 years, which means He had to have had some color to His fleshly skin. Does it matter what color that was? Why make such a big deal about it? In fact, aren't we spiritually race-baiting by even bringing up these sorts of questions?

You may feel uncomfortable with this subject, and you might feel yourself bridling at the concepts and feelings and thoughts these words might be conjuring in your mind, but at least hear me out before you close the book and write me off. Come with me on this journey. Fasten your seatbelt and hold on. There will be some turbulence ahead in these pages, but know that we will land in the arms of a loving God who so loves each and every one of us that He sent us His only begotten Son, who loves us each of *exactly the way we are.*

There is an old song that says, "It is no secret what God can do. What He's done for others, He'll do for you."[16] I live under the healing grace of God, who is healing me. I am recovering from the hurt, the embarrassment, the doubt, the low self-esteem and flawed self-image that a racist society has forced on me. But I am *not a mistake* any more than you are. You were not born the wrong or right color; you are an intentional object of the love of God, which means every one of us was born with the perfect color.

I used to be suspicious of everybody with a white face because of the way that man at that ship talked to my daddy that day. Every time I think I'm over it, somebody like that woman down there in Dallas who tossed her keys to me and told me to park her car comes

---

16  "It Is No Secret (What God Can Do)"; a hymn written by Jim Reeves. Source: LyricFind

up to me, and I have a flashback. Or that flight attendant who warned me in Chicago that I was standing in the first-class line—where I actually belonged.

Day by day I trust the Lord for my healing. Day by day I strain to forget those things which are behind me and press on to all God has called me to. I pray the same for you, that you would go forth in the healing power of God so that your life will be a testimony of God's healing power. You are on a journey of wholeness, health, and healing. You will be an example of the Lord our Healer to all you encounter. So, go forth, and in your healing, let God use you to heal others.

Okay, buckle up, and let's get to it.

# 2
# WELCOME TO THE WAR

*"Racism is the dogma that one ethnic group is condemned by nature to congenital inferiority and another group is destined to congenital superiority."*
—**Ruth Benedict**, *Race: Science and Politics*[17]

*I was social chairman, so I decided we would go ahead with the frat party. I felt that what we all needed was to try to lighten up in the midst of the shock and deep sadness of losing Dr. King to the finality of such sudden racial violence.*

*The Alpha House was on one side of the campus and, separated by the quad, my girlfriend was on the other side of the campus in her room at Alpha Kappa Alpha Sorority. I set out across the quad to get her and walk her back to Alpha House for the party.*

*No way could I have known that within minutes we would be funneled to a gauntlet of snarling police dogs barely constrained by their chains, held loosely by a phalanx of nervous, shouting, armed cops with guns unsnapped and batons raised...*

\* \* \*

The Bible uses various terms to refer to Christians. Followers of Christ were first called "Christians" in Antioch (Acts 11:26). These followers were also called disciples, believers, saints, the faithful, and brothers and sisters in the Lord. According to the *Evangelical Dictionary of Biblical Theology*:

---

17   Ruth Fulton Benedict (1887-1948); *Science and Politics*, ©1940, Viking Compass Books.

"The New Testament contains over 175 names, descriptive titles, and figures of speech referring to Christians, applicable to both the individual and the group. The origin of these names is traceable to the Old Testament, Jesus' teaching, the church, and nonbelievers."[18]

One of the Pauline monikers for Christians is "soldier." He writes his son Timothy with the voice of a soon-to-retire general in the army of the Lord, encouraging his young lieutenant rookie officer, to be a good soldier (2 Timothy 2:3-4). This image of the believer is in line with his exhortation to the church at Ephesus, where he instructs the brethren there to don the whole armor of God as one entering warfare. As that great British prince of preachers, Charles Spurgeon, says: "We are soldiers of the King of kings."[19] The late gospel artist Walter Hawkins put it lyrically and musically:

> *There's a war going on*
> *And if you're gonna win*
> *You better make sure that you have Jesus deep down within*
> *This battle cannot be won with bullets and guns*
> *For the enemy you cannot see with human faculties*[20]

There is a war going on. Make no mistake about it. It's a war between the divine and the demonic. Between light and darkness. The celestial and the terrestrial. This war is ravaging nations, countries, economies, neighborhoods, and entire families. It is a war of bias and prejudice and racism. A war of separation and division. A war that is often debated, often discussed, and all too often only minimally resolved—and even that's an exaggeration. It is a war that

---

18  *Evangelical Dictionary of Biblical Theology*, ©1996, Baker Books. All rights reserved. Used by permission.

19  *Encyclopedia of Illustrations* by Charles Spurgeon. Biblesoft Formatted Electronic Database © 2015 by Biblesoft, Inc. All rights reserved.

20  "There's A War Going On," lyrics by Walter Hawkins. See: https://www.azlyrics.com/lyrics/walterhawkins/theresawargoingon.html

in many cases the church has either been AWOL or encamped on the wrong side. It is a race war that is not of God and that is, at its core, pure *sin*.

If this war over race, this deliberate separation based on cultures and ethnicities, is not of God, what does He say about it? What is God's agenda? What are our marching orders in this war?

There are some things I believe the Lord wants us to see that too many of us are just not getting. Some of those things are tough, complicated, even complex. But I come not from the perspective of an anthropologist or a sociologist or a historian or even an activist. I take the posture of a student of the Word of God. We each should take the stance not of experts or theologians or scholars, but of students eager to hear and learn what our Creator has to say on the topic of racism.

There was a group in the Bible called the Bereans. These were people who searched the Scriptures to see what the Word says. To make a panoramic view of the totality of the will of God, it's important to look at the beginning, the middle, and the end. To just see what commentary the Word of God, the plan of God, the mind of God, gives from the very beginning, then into these middle times, and moving eschatologically to the end times or times yet to come.

Laying a foundation of the Word, let's look at Acts chapter 17. What was God's plan from the beginning? "And he hath made of one blood all nations." One version says made "of one man." All nations; one blood. "Made of one blood, all nations of men to dwell on all the face of the earth"—that is, scattered throughout the earth—"and hath determined the times before appointed, and the bounds and their habitation." In other words, God made all of mankind from just *one*. We're all of one blood. Every human being when cut bleeds red, no matter the color on the outside. That was God's original plan: from one comes many. And so, from the beginning, God's plan was that He made mankind from one blood.

Now to the middle times, Galatians 3:28, where I believe God's plan is right now in history, the present-day agenda: "There is neither Jew nor Greek"—one version says *Jew nor Gentile*—"neither slave nor free, neither male nor female, for you are all one in Christ." So, there is this unity. From the beginning, it was a unity of blood. We are all one in Christ. In these middle times we are especially unified by our relationship with Christ. So here we are. All one in Christ by creation. Therefore, the church, if no other element in society, should be a demonstration of unity, and unity with diversity, and diversity in that unity. We are one as a demonstration of the plan of God.

So, how does this oneness thing end up? For the answer to that, let's jump to the end, the book of Revelation, and take a look at a few verses. Revelation 5:9 says, speaking of Jesus, "And they sang a new song: You are worthy to take the scroll and to open its seals, because you were slain, and with your blood you purchased for God persons from every tribe, every language and people and nation." So, the people of God are from every tribe, nation, every tongue.

Now to Revelation 7:9, "After this I looked, and there before me was a great multitude coming up from every nation and no one could count them, from every nation, every tribe, every people, every language, standing before the throne and before the Lamb, and they were wearing white robes and they were holding palm branches in their hands," emphasizing victory.

Now to Revelation 5:14, "The four living creatures said, Amen. And the elders fell and worshiped." They triumphed. They took victory over the enemy. Another way to say it is this: "They conquered the enemy by the blood of the lamb and by the word of their testimony; and they did not love their lives so much as to shrink from death."

Here's what we have: in the end times, heaven will be inhabited by every race, every creed, every color, every nation, every tongue, every language. Not a couple, not a few, not just some of these and some of those. *All. Every.*

I wonder. If I look down on someone here on earth, where am I going when all the saints will be together in heaven? Do I think I'm going with the non-haters to a place where discord and division and separation are not allowed? If you don't like me here on earth, where are you going when all the saints join together in heaven, where haters and discord and division and separation are not allowed? We may call out to Jesus as the gates of heaven are being shut to us, "Lord, Lord, did I not speak in your name and go to church and pray?" but if we harbor malice and sow discord and support racial separation and disparage God's children, all due to their skin color, should we really expect to be counted among those who honor God's Word?

Don't bet on it.

There's an emphasis on unity in the eternal plan of God and it involves all believers and clearly lays out the dos and the don'ts. No spirit-filled church can tolerate, allow, or maintain an atmosphere of racism. Let that simmer for a moment. We cannot maintain, abide, or permit such an atmosphere. We cannot wink at it. We cannot play games with an atmosphere that acknowledges and accepts, or intentionally overlooks, a spirit of racism. *It is anti-God.* Which, put another way, is anti-Christ. Think on *that* for a moment. You serve the will and the spirit of antichrist when you sow or allow racial disunity among God's creations—whether they are believers or not. Because *all* are God's.

God's plan is that we all came from one blood and, therefore, from one blood, from one man, the earth would be filled. How will the earth be filled with God's glory if they're not people who declare His glory? God says that those declaring His glory in every part of the world shall be of every tribe, every nation, every tongue, every language. That means there are people who don't look like you at all—and that's a part of God's perfect plan. The divisions and the breaches and breaks and schisms do not exist in the Kingdom. We are all one. When Jesus prayed His last prayer, He said, "Lord, make them one."

Hence, it is sin, it is antithetical to the Word of God, if racism is espoused, expressed, and tolerated. We are all one in the Lord. Jeremiah the prophet said it. Isaiah the prophet said it. Ezekiel the prophet said it. We are all one in the Lord, and one in the Kingdom of God.

Now let's go to the book of Colossians, chapter 2, so we can look at this issue from the perspective of a military motif. Colossians 2:8 says, "See to it"—one version says *beware*; another says *be on the lookout*—"that no one takes you captive through hollow and deceptive philosophy." The phrase "take you captive" is a military term of those who are captured in battle. In other words, do not become a prisoner of war.[21] This is a warfare of the mind, of unspiritual, ungodly philosophies shaped by the world systems that are deceptive, hollow and void of the priorities, principles and values of the Kingdom of God. The idea is of a person who has been "kidnapped," taken prisoner—in this case, gotten captured by the opposing side, by the enemy of the unity of the Kingdom.

The Bible is warning us to make sure we don't become a prisoner of war, particularly through hollow and deceptive philosophies. It's the same idea that we can be made captive by the mindset of the culture, which can, if we aren't aware, captivate us through human tradition. It is not a Word of God. It is a creation of man. It is the philosophy of man and certain elemental spiritual forces of this world, rather than one of Christ. In other words, be careful that no one takes you captive through values, standards, and ethics that represent empty deceit based on human tradition and the elemental forces of the world, and not based on Christ and God's Word."[22]

Colossians 2, verse 10 adds, "And in Christ you have been brought to fullness. He is the head over every power and authority."

21  *The Bible Exposition Commentary* (1989), by Chariot Victor Publishing, and imprint of Cook Communication Ministries. All rights reserved. Used by permission.
22  *The Apologetics Study Bible*, Copyright © 2007 by Holman Bible Publishers. All Rights Reserved.

And verse 15: "And having disarmed the powers and authorities, He made a public spectacle of them, triumphing over them by the cross." These are terms about principalities, powers and authorities, alluding to Ephesians chapter 6, which tells us that we wrestle not against flesh and blood, but against entities and spiritual wickedness in high places, principalities and powers, agents of the demonic enemies of Almighty God.

The whole race issue is encased in spiritual warfare. Racism is not of God. It's a stronghold devised by the devil, who plagues literally all our culture and society. It's an area, a dimension, a "cultural turf" the enemy has commandeered, cordoned off, set up walls around, and taken control of. From the beginning, the middle and the end, it's contrary to the very will of God.

Recently, the subject of spiritual warfare has been linked to the political climate in America. It appears that theology, sociology, and politics have become intertwined in these "last and evil days" (as some of my Pentecostal friends would say). In his commentary in the October 2019 edition of the conservative magazine *Charisma,* founder and author Stephen Strang cites a prayer given by Pastor Paula White Cain on the occasion of the announcement by President Trump that he would run for re-election. Strang notes that Pastor Paula prayed:

"Father, You have raised President Trump up for such a time as this. And invoked biblical blessings while coming against 'principalities and powers.'" She continues, "Let every evil veil of deception of the enemy be removed from people's eyes in the name which is above every name, the name of Jesus Christ....You said in Your Word...in Ephesians 6:12, that 'We are not wrestling against flesh and blood but against principalities, powers, against rulers of darkness of this world against spiritual wickedness in high places ...So right now, let every demonic network that has aligned itself against the purpose, against the calling of President Trump, let it be broken. Let it be torn down in the name of Jesus. Let the counsel of the wicked be spoiled right now, according to Job 12:1....I deploy the hand of God to work for him in the name of Jesus. I secure his calling. I secure his purpose. I secure his family. And we secure victory in the name which is above every name, the name that has never failed for this nation, and for my life, the name of Jesus Christ. And everybody said, Amen.'"[23]

Now, I wonder if certain other church leaders and theologians and Christian leaders prayed the same about previous presidents, that they were "raised up for such a time as this." Did they pray that for President Obama, that God ordained that he be the U.S. President for such a time as that in which he was in the White House, or did Mr. Obama somehow sneak by God's will and plan? Did they pray of President Obama for God to "let every demonic network that has aligned itself against the purpose, against the calling of President Obama be broken"? How about President Jimmy Carter? Or do certain U.S. Presidents not qualify for such prayer because they're not of the right color or party? It's just a question. I hope all professed leaders, pastors, preachers and teachers prayed *for* President Obama and *for* President Carter and others with whom they may have politically or otherwise disagreed. If they truly are men and women of God, they probably did pray the same for previous American presidents, for we are all one, says the Lord.

In his article, Mr. Strang goes on to say, "It's a daily battle the enemy wages in our personal lives, in our homes, in our cities, and even in Washington."[24]

As I was writing this, I did an experiment; I Googled the phrase "Trump and race spiritual warfare." I found it very interesting that some of the headlines the search engine cited are

---

23  Stephen Strang. Article: "Spiritual Warfare, Contemporary Culture and Politics: Paula White Cain's spiritual-warfare prayer at a Trump rally was exactly what America needed." *Charisma*, October 2019. Pg. 58.
24  Ibid.

no longer available. Maybe the posting merely expired. Or maybe
it's part of the ever-increasing media-wars, philosophical wars
and political wars that plague the climate of the country, because
it appears that in some camps, phrases like "race wars" are being
replaced with "spiritual warfare." Which indicates that we had
better learn who the real enemy is, or we'll go after the wrong side
all while thinking we're in the right.

Clearly there is division across the political aisle, but during the
tenure of our current president, many (especially on the conservative
side of the political and ecclesiastical divide) are identifying the
times with spiritual language. This whole idea, this whole battle,
this fight, this history, is all birthed out of a demonic mindset. We
mustn't sugarcoat that. As long as there is widespread denial of the
spiritual dimension of our alienated times, we will at best be limited
in addressing and correcting it, and at the worst inadequate and even
powerless to make things better between that which separates and
divides us. Our distinctions will remain divisions and our divisions
will remain walls. And don't hang in all on, "Well, we all make
mistakes," because that's just another lie, a way of softening our
responses to an insidious attitude in the midst of a deadly war.

Don't rationalize sin. Don't rationalize ungodliness. Call it
what it is. Call it out. Repent of it, turn from it, and make things
better, based on what God has said. Racism is not of God. Hear me
on this one: It is not of God.

*Racism is sin.*

At significant points in history, such as *today*, the church has
been willfully complicit in fostering the spiritual dimension to the
racial, spiritual and even cultural animosity that is the painful reality
of our society. Not only has the church often been AWOL—absent
altogether—but much of the church has defected, joined the enemy,
and taken up a posture and position that is contrary to the very Word
and will of God. It's clearly evident when one not only watches what

self-proclaimed Christians say these days, but what they *do*. And shall we not know a true Christian by what they *do*—how they treat others, take care of the needy, reach out to the disenfranchised, help the poor, aid the displaced, comfort the broken?

Jesus prayed in John 17:21-22, *Lord, make them one.* May they be unified. He's saying make them one, right there in that room with twelve guys who could not have been more different. God says, Make them one, yet the church itself, who should be on the front lines in this way, has often been on the side of the enemy, contributing to the disregard, the delay, the destruction of the unity for which our Lord prayed. You don't have to believe me, but what I'm writing comes strictly from God's Word.

In America, the church must face the reality of its historical participation in marginalizing "the other." Indeed, around the world, cultures have devolved in societies, nations, countries, neighborhoods and governments to the point of often being part of the reality of marginality. In other words, there has been a distinct and systematic way of handling those placed or positioned or pushed to the margins, while keeping those in the margins *inside* those margins, thereby increasingly ignoring how marginalized, disengaged and disenfranchised they are. It's an insidious, vicious downward spiral that, at its end, fails to categorize some groups as even human, caging some groups because of who they or their parents are, forcing others to live outside of the norms of shelter even in the wealthiest democracies, shoving still others into squalid camps to "protect" them from those who would do them further harm—while allowing them to be harmed in those very camps.

What have we become? I do realize the Bible says that in the end times the hearts of many will grow cold, but have we arrived in those times already? Have we truly lost all concern for those who need us most—even those we categorize as "unsaved" (and who we should look at as "future Christians")?

Recall the day of Pentecost in Acts chapter 2. The power of the Holy Spirit came when the 120 people were inside the room with the doors locked. Yet, what happened in the room could not remain in the room; it spilled out all over the streets of Jerusalem and eventually 5,000 people were saved. The thing that caught their attention was that the people inside the room who were Jews were speaking in tongues and in other languages. Chapter 2, verse 7, contains a clue to the issue of marginality: upon hearing these Jews speaking in foreign languages, "They were utterly amazed. They asked, 'Aren't these Galileans?'"

The question that arose in their minds was, *I thought these guys were Galileans?* Why would that be an issue? Those in attendance, upon hearing the Jews speaking in foreign tongues, did not ask, "Hey, aren't these guys Ethiopians? Aren't these Cappadocians? Aren't these Mesopotamians?" No. Their question was, "Aren't these men Galileans?"

Why did they ask that? Galilee was a region in northern Israel. Jerusalem, where this had first occurred in the upper room, was in southern Israel. At the time this took place, in and around Jerusalem were people from all over the world .(Acts 2:5 describes it as, "God-fearing Jews from every nation under heaven.") Yet, no one said, "Hey, are these people speaking the language of Libya, in northern Africa?" Never asked that. The question was, *are they Galileans?* Why is that significant? Because from Jerusalem going north, you go through Samaria. On the other side of Samaria is the region of Galilee. Included in Galilee is a place called Nazareth. It's pretty far north of Jerusalem. In fact, Galilee is a place of marginality.

This happened once before. Go to Luke chapter 23. Jesus is before Pilate. Luke 23:6, "On hearing this, Pilate asked if this man was a Galilean." *This Jesus guy,* Pilate wants to know, *all those miracles y'all said he did, is he from Galilee? Is he a Galilean?* What was going on here? Why was everyone asking about Galilee?

It happened again in Matthew 26:69. Jesus is hanging on the cross. Disciples are leaving one by one. One of the last to leave is Peter. As he's sitting outside in the courtyard, he's approached by a little servant girl who asks him, "Weren't you one of those guys with Jesus of Galilee?" She didn't ask, "Hey, weren't you with Jesus of Nazareth?" Didn't want to know if he was with Jesus of Jerusalem. No, it was always *Galilee*, a place on the fringe, on the margins, out in the sticks, the boonies, across the tracks. Indeed, it would become known later in history as *Galilee of the Gentiles*—a place of marginalization.[25] This is why one of the pre-apostles could so comfortably have said, "Can any good thing come out of Nazareth?"—which was in Galilee.

*The Dictionary of Jesus* and the Gospels describes it this way: "Inhabitants of Jerusalem regarded Galilee as a backward locale (cf. Acts 2:7), peculiar first of all because of its dialect (Matthew 26:73), in which laryngeal sounds were swallowed."[26]

Here's the point: Jesus was an outsider, a Galilean, a man from the margins of society. The woman asked Peter if he knew Jesus, identifying Jesus as a Galilean, and she recognized Peter by the way he talked. He had an ethnic dialectic that was recognizable, and she recognized him by his language. She approached Peter (and she might not have been the first, because everybody started noticing him) and he cussed her out for openly putting him on the spot, identifying him with a Galilean "criminal" who was charged with causing a big uproar. The identification was as a Galilean. Galileans were in the margins of society.

Included in that margins list of nations was Asia, which was the home of people in the margins even though they were present at the Day of Pentecost. Marginalized Asia is where Ephesus is—

---

25  Unger, M. F., Harrison, R. K., Vos, H. F., Barber, C. J., & Unger, M. F.; *Unger's Bible Dictionary* (1988), in an article titled "Galilee." *The new Unger's Bible Dictionary*. Revision of: Unger's Bible dictionary. 3rd ed. c1966. (Rev. and updated ed.). Chicago: Moody Press.
26  *Dictionary of Jesus and the Gospels*, ©1992 by InterVarsity Christian Fellowship/USA. All rights reserved.

today's eastern Turkey. In the beginning of the book of Revelations, Asia Minor is where the seven churches are located. Most of the travels of Paul were in Asia because the home base had moved from Jerusalem to Antioch, and from Antioch out to the uttermost parts of the world. And the uttermost parts of the world were considered the marginalized fringes.

## More than Black and White

Isn't it interesting that the Bible clearly says Asians were there on the Day of Pentecost? As the church began to spread, it spread first through Asia. It's also interesting that seldomly today do we hear discussions about racism and bias that includes Asians. How often do we hear front-line arguments, discussions, or debates about racism that includes Asians? I would venture to say far less so than blacks and Hispanics.

The discrimination debate in America has been primarily framed as black against white, yet it is a part of the very strategy of the enemy that certain marginalized groups not be included in the discussion, even though they experience the same realities of marginalization. It is a subtle, satanic strategy that conversations about racism, for the most part, ignore the fact that Asians have also been discriminated against and are part of a racist mindset. There were Asians at Pentecost. The first church grew in Asia. Yet, there has been discrimination in this country against Asians, just as there has been discrimination against blacks and Hispanics.

On December 7, 1947, the Japanese bombed Pearl Harbor. From that infamous event, Franklin Roosevelt passed a law that imprisoned all Asians, whether they were born in the U.S. or not. I never learned that when I was in school. I have been in school all my life, and I never heard that in any history lesson or sociology class (though I realize it's being taught in schools nowadays). Yet, even today, Asians are not included all that much in discussions about racism.

But there was a point in history in this nation when that was not so. They were not only discussed, they were illegally imprisoned. Japanese internment camps were the 20th century version of slavery against Asians. Nobody talks about that much these days. Racism involving African Americans dominates the debates and discussions about this sensitive issue, while racism involving Asian-Americans is, at best, seen as an anecdote, an isolated historical anomaly, even though thousands were interned.

In his excellent work, *From a Liminal Place: An Asian American Theology*, Sang H. Lee states:

> "...Anti-Asian American racism is not taken seriously (because) incidents of anti-Asian American discrimination are usually thought of as 'isolated discrimination.' 'Isolated discrimination' is defined as 'harmful action taken intentionally by a member of a dominant group against members of a subordinate racial or ethnic group without being socially embedded in the larger organizational or community context.' Isolated discrimination is then distinguished from such large-scale and organized acts of discrimination as the Chinese Exclusion Act of 1882, the Asian Exclusion Act of 1924, and the internment of Japanese and Japanese American citizens in 1942. 'Isolated discrimination,' then, is taken to be 'isolated incidents' and therefore not really significant. But are the incidents of isolated discrimination really so isolated and thus not really significant? Personally, when I have encountered such isolated incidents of discrimination, I could not dismiss them as unimportant."[27]

Far be it for minorities to compare the sufferings of their degradation and discrimination with others. It is a mute argument

---

27  Sang H. Lee, *From a Liminal Place: An Asian American Theology* (p. 16). Fortress Press. Kindle Edition.

to debate whether the Holocaust was more devastating to the Jews than slavery was to the African Americans than forced internment was to Asians. It is a futile debate to take sides as to whether the chains of plantation slavery were more painful than the chains of Japanese internment camps of World War II. Lee continues:

> "The complexity of the issues of justice and reconciliation is nowhere more apparent than in the case of the U.S. internment of Japanese American residents and citizens during World War II. In the midst of the hysteria created by the Japanese attack on Pearl Harbor on December 7, 1941, the U.S. government, under Executive Order 9066, blatantly violated the Constitution by forcibly evacuating 120,000 Japanese residents and American-born Japanese American citizens out of their homes and businesses and by imprisoning them in hurriedly constructed so-called relocation centers located in uninhabited, desolate areas of several western states. The magnitude and depth of the pain and shame that this 'concentration camp' experience inflicted upon the internees will probably never be completely understood."[28]

Not to mention the violence perpetrated against Mexicans, who had most of the northern half of their nation confiscated by U.S. military action and were turned essentially into America's permanent servant class.

The second strategy that operates on those at the margins is division. First deceit. Then division.

On April 29, 1992, the city of Los Angeles was thrust into one of the greatest tragedies in its history. It began with a black man named Rodney King being savagely beaten with batons by

---

28  Ibid. P169

several white police officers on March 4, 1991. King's crime? He was speeding.

Why would speeding and even attempting to elude officers have compelled the officers to fracture his eye socket, break his cheekbone and leg, and smash bones at the base of his neck in eleven places? Officers said he was speeding and that when he finally did pull over, he was combative and noncompliant, acted like he was under the influence of drugs, and appeared to be reaching for a weapon. Videotape of the incident showed otherwise. King had no weapon, toxicological tests later revealed no PCP in his system, and in the videotape of him being beaten by the half dozen cops, he appeared compliant and passive. And the officers were unaware of his police record until after they finished pummeling him.[29]

In spite of the devastation in the wake of this uprising, within a matter of weeks the story faded from the headlines, which shifted to the story of conflict between Koreans and blacks in the inner city. Thirteen days after the videotaped beating of Rodney King was initially aired, a 15 year-old African American girl named Latasha Harlins was shot to death by a female Korean convenience store owner. The woman was eventually sentenced to a fine of $500 and 400 hours of community service, but no prison time. Harlins' crime? Videotape of that incident revealed that the store owner had yelled at her, yanked her by the sweater, and Harlins turned and hit her. The store owner fell down, came back up with a stool, threw it at her, reached beneath the counter and pulled out a handgun. Harlins put a bottle on the counter while the store owner fumbled with the gun, then turned and walked toward the exit. The store owner shouted at her and fired the weapon. The bullet struck Harlins in the back of the head.[30]

It is believed that the combination of the vivid images of the

---

29  Paraphrased from *Slipping Into Darkness: A True Story from the American Ghetto*, chapter 2; by M. Rutledge McCall (Archangel House books; 2001).

30  Ibid.

vicious beating of Rodney King in early March, coupled with the videotape of teenaged Latasha Harlins less than two weeks later, added to the outrage. This led to a bloody war sparked from the flashpoint on the corner of Western Street and Florence Avenue (the same street a few blocks south in South Central where the church I pastor is located) just hours after the verdict in the trial of the police officers who beat Rodney King exonerated them. The intersection of Florence and Normandy became fertile ground that brought forth a devastating crop of hatred and laid 58 bodies in coffins by the time it was over.

It is notable, however, that despite the seemingly senseless destruction of billions of dollars worth of property in African American neighborhoods by predominantly African Americans, the lingering story was the vitriolic animosity and hatred that continued brewing between two marginalized communities: the black community and the Korean community, but stereotypically at different ends of the economic spectrum.

Asian theology says that Asians have been designated as the "middle of minority." Others call it the model minority. What does all that mean? It means that Asians are played against other minorities in a culture that simultaneously lifts up Asians as models of success while putting them down for being Asian. Therefore, when someone says there's no issue of racism, the model that is often used to validate that assertion is Asians—who are then pitted against blacks and other persons of color.

Sang Hyun Lee speaks of the peculiar juxtaposition between Asians and other marginalized races, calling it:

"...the myth of Asian Americans as the so-called model minority. This myth, disseminated widely by the mass media, holds that the economic and educational successes of many Asian immigrants prove that they are not really discriminated against and that America is still a land of opportunity. The 'model minority' idea has many problems. It draws people's attention to those Asian

American young people who have gone to Ivy League schools and to the success of some Asian immigrant small-business establishments. What it ignores, however, are such realities as the heavy involvement of multiple family members in these Asian immigrant small businesses (which often includes a punishing fourteen- to sixteen-hour workday), which makes their per capita income much lower than that of white laborers. The concept also ignores many Asian immigrant youth who experience severe psychological problems in coping with their deeply alienated predicament."[31]

Citing the political analysis of the marginalization of Asians, Sang Hyun Lee refers to sociologists Won Moo Hurh and Wesley Woo, who suggest that Asians join the ranks of other people of color as victims of institutional racism while being postured as the "model minority," serves as another tool of manipulation to enhance the goal of division among the disenfranchised with the following goals:

"(1) exclusion of Asian Americans from social programs supported by public and private agencies (benefit-denying/fund-saving function); (2) disguise of Asian Americans' underemployment (institutional racism promoting function); (3) justification of the American open social system (system preserving function); (4) displacement of the system's fault to less-achieving minorities (victim blaming function); and (5) anti-Asian sentiment and activities (resentment reinforcing function)."[32]

In my experience, Asians have been held up as "super-minorities." I've always known they were different, like I am, but not "as different" as I am. They were the American success stories. They came here with nothing (as the tale is often told) and rose to the top of the heap. Well, almost to the top, but certainly higher than blacks and Hispanics. Being Asian, they were assumed to be smart

---

31  Lee, Sang Hyun. *From a Liminal Place: Asian American Theology.* Minneapolis: Fortress Press Location 97 of 4099, Kindle Edition.

32  Lee, Sang H. *From a Liminal Place: An Asian American Theology* (p. 14). Fortress Press. Kindle Edition.

(another stereotype), just like blacks who were always told they had to work harder, study longer, and do twice as much as the white kids and the Asian kids. They were always higher on the pole than we blacks and Hispanics. So goes the "model minority" theory.

We always saw both whites and Asians as the "competition." I believe that idea was in the mix during the Korean/black race wars in South Los Angeles from the mid-1960s through the L.A. riot of 1992, where businesses in inner-city neighborhoods were dominated by a few white, many Asian, and virtually no black businesspeople. In those South Central neighborhoods, Asians were the closest obvious cultural targets, due to the dearth of Caucasians on which to vent one's race-based frustrations. Lee attempts to explain this:

> "...Sometimes [it's] hard to talk about racism against Asian Americans [due to] the present-day American situation of the white-black paradigm in the common discourse—a discourse in which the experiences of Asian Americans as a 'middle minority,' a buffer people between the whites and the blacks, are often trivialized and dismissed ....That marginalization of Asians, in fact, within a black and white racial formation, "disciplines" both Asian Americans and Asians and constitutes the essential site of Asian American oppression. By seeing only black and white, the presence and absence of all color, whites render Asians, American Indians, and Latinos invisible, ignoring the gradations and complexities of the full spectrum between the racial poles."[33]

I served for about eight years on the academic affairs committee of the Board of Trustees at Biola University near Orange County in Southern California. We were required to

---

33   Ibid, pg. 15

report our ethnic numbers to the academic authorities on a regular basis. Biola ranked very high in its minority numbers. Yet, I was the only chocolate person on the board, and we had very low numbers in our African American student body.

I told a friend on the finance committee that Biola was one of the best-kept secrets in Los Angeles, because it was a Christian university that was virtually unknown on my side of town. As long as I had been on the board, as far as I knew, the president of Biola had never come to "the 'hood'" of South Los Angeles. Biola never even significantly recruited up the road on the black side of town, either. But I noticed that three or four times a year the president of Biola would travel to Korea.

I asked my friend why the school had little or no presence in South Los Angeles, even though our president went back and forth to Asia.

My friend responded straight-faced, "Ken, it's just business."

In my mind, I heard the words of the Godfather, Don Corleone, from the Mario Puzo novel, *It's nothing personal. It's only business. Fahgeddabout it.*

"What do you mean?" I asked him, wondering what kind of business could be better had from thousands of miles away than from right under our noses.

"It costs us to go to Watts," he explained. "When the president goes to Korea, he comes back with potential students who pay cash. If we go recruiting students from Watts, we have to raise money for scholarships. It's cheaper to go to Korea."

The culture plays one against the other, so not only do Asians seem to be the middle minority, they're seen as the *model* middle minority. "Why can't y'all be like them?" too many black kids hear about their Asian peers.

Sub-marginalization among the marginalized divides, separates, and conquers them. It's a depraved game, and the devil entices many to play it well.

## The Deprivation of Division

We've looked at the deceit of racism and the division of racism;now let's take a look at the deprivation in the mix. The farther people are at the margins of society, the less access they have to the resources that exist at the core of the culture. The power, authority, and resources under the control of the small core of the dominant culture invariably remain out of the reach of the marginalized, who are systematically deprived of access, or given only limited access, to the fullness of the benefits thereof.

We must realize that we are in a war—indeed, a generational war. Babies are not born disliking other kids because of their color. Babies don't fight over ethnicity. They fight over toys. Racism is taught. Children absorb what's around them: what they see, hear, observe, and often experience. Prejudice is an ungodly mindset that is taught and passed from one generation to the next.

It's a war in the spirit realm, and we must not allow it to take our children as victims. We must declare that it cannot have our families. It cannot have generations to come. It cannot have our culture, cannot have our businesses, cannot have our schools, cannot have our homes. Cannot have our *minds*. We're in a war here, and it must stop.

The Bible speaks of victory in spiritual warfare in Revelation 12:11 where it says that we shall "overcome by the blood of the lamb" (NKJV). As a witness pleads the fifth amendment as authority not to speak against him or herself, we must plead the blood of Jesus as our authority to speak victory over every element of racism and bias and discrimination and prejudice. We must individually stand as an army of one, yet combine our voices and with one spirit declare the defeat of the demonic enemy called racism—in any form.

Make a declaration that if it doesn't happen anywhere else,

it's going to start right in your house. There are enough people reading this book right now to make a difference. There are enough of us to go out into the highways and byways of our fractured and fragmented world and stand boldly, and tell somebody to tell somebody to tell somebody else that racism is not of God and you/I/we declare war on it.

In the words of the contemporary gospel troubadour Charles Jenkins in the song "This Means War," this is a declaration that begins with you as an individual, an army of one person. On a personal, practical level, it means that you recognize that you don't have to stay on the bottom because somebody assigned you to the bottom. You don't have to stay without because someone says you aren't within, you don't measure up, or you don't have "it." You're not "in." You are made to be on the top, not the bottom. God makes no mistakes. He's not biased toward one over another.

You have the power in you to bind every spirit of racism and division that comes against you or anyone else. It is not merely a metaphysical, pseudo-religious incantation, but a practical, cognitive decision to stand against racism—blatant or camouflaged. Speak the breaking of the bonds of memories that take you back to what happened somewhere in your past, to what happened to your family, what happened to your ancestors, or to your friends. Bring down any mindset or idea of racism. Speak it over your life in the name of Jesus. Speak healing of past hurts. Speak healing of generational offenses. Speak healing over your house.

Declare that this is war, and you're joining it.

# 3
# RACISM IN BLACK AND WHITE

*"The Bible contains no narratives in which the original intent was
to negate the full humanity of black people or view blacks in an
unfavorable way. Such negative attitudes about black people are
entirely postbiblical."*
**—Dr. Cain Hope Felder,** *Stoney The Road We Trod* [34]

*I strode calmly across the quad to pick up my girl at the AKA
house for the party back at APA.*

*On our way back to Alpha House, we decided to stop in at the
Student Union and invite any black faces we came across to join the
party at the house. We entered through the inside entrance off the
quad and had been there only a handful of minutes when we heard
a startling commotion, followed by shattering glass, and then police
sirens and people shouting and screaming.*

*The back lobby of the Union was suddenly flooded with black
faces, people running hysterically, trying to get out of the building
only to be caught and cut off by cops in riot gear with billy clubs
swinging...*

\* \* \*

Racism is an equal opportunity employer. It knows no
boundaries. It is a pervasive synthesis of issues related to color,
social status, and political and economic power. Regardless of the
seeming limitations of the discussion that would confine it to the

---

34   Felder, Cain Hope, editor. *Stoney The Road We Trod: African American Biblical Interpretations.* Minneapolis: Fortress Press 1991. Pg. 127.

relationship between blacks and whites, racism is far bigger than that. For example, there are often issues in the east between Koreans and Japanese and Chinese. If we broaden our definition to include ethnic differences, we would notice a peculiar relationship between Hispanic groups and the not so subtle biases among those who speak a common Spanish language or come from one of several Latino heritages.

A few years ago, in an attempt to be more inclusive and sensitive to the changing ethnic makeup of greater Los Angeles, my church held a Cinco de Mayo celebration whereupon I immediately proceeded to make several mistakes. First, I thought May 5 was the date of Mexico's independence from Spain, much like America's independence from Great Britain on July 4. I was wrong. Several Columbian and Central American Latino members of my church tactfully corrected my inaccurate understanding of history. Cinco de Mayo was not the Mexican day of independence, and Mexico's independence day was nowhere near the month of May.

Cinco de Mayo celebrates an underdog Mexican army that defeated France in the Battle of Puebla in 1862. Not only was it not a war for independence, but the victory was short-lived when France came back a few years later and occupied Mexico all over again. The actual Mexican Independence Day is celebrated on September 16, honoring the day in 1810 when a priest named Miguel Hidalgo implored Mexico to revolt against Spain, leading to the War for Independence which ended in 1821.[35]

During my discovery process, I learned that some of the Latino worshipers at our church were a bit offended to be lumped into the category of Mexican-American. I would later learn that there was often animosity among some former island dwellers or

---

35  *New York Times* article by Claudio E. Cabrera and Louis Lucero II. May 5, 2018, See: https://www.nytimes.com/2018/05/05/business/cinco-de-mayo-facts-history.html and: http://www.pbs.org/kera/usmexicanwar/biographies/hildago_costilla.html and: https://www.history.com/this-day-in-history/mexican-war-of-independence-begins

those from central or South America, and that even native speakers of Spanish felt little or no kindred spirit toward Mexicans born in Mexico and held little reverence for days celebrated by Mexican-Americans. This might be considered quasi-racism, as it is a bias against a group with whom you have commonalities; in this case a common language.

So, racism can be much more pervasive than merely dark or light skin, geographic location, or a different nation or religion. And it's been around for a long time. It will take someone like you and me to draw a line in the sand and say *no more*, because our culture has marginalized parts of itself.

Yet, it's interesting that even from the margins theology arises. More interestingly, those who have been marginalized ask theological questions about the God who was the same yesterday, today, and forever. For example, black theology grew out of the marginalization of African Americans. In other words, a theology that addresses the cultural, sociological position of African Americans emerged from state-sanctioned marginality of their culture. However, though we were pushed to the corners and margins of society, God was still at work.

That the Word of God was involved in this theological marginalization could only have taken place through human error, deliberate or otherwise. The revelation of the historical engagement of God was founded upon an assumption of error with a hermeneutic of suspicion—a fancy way of describing the interpretation of Scripture with a suspicion that "maybe this passage isn't really what they told me it says, and maybe it says more than they told me it says, and maybe it means more than they told me it means." In other words, the premise is that it's possible certain interpretations of Scripture don't tell the whole story.

One of my mentors, Dr. Cain Hope Felder, is the former dean of the School of Divinity at Howard University. Dr. Felder formed a theory called the Theory of Sacralization and Secularization. This theological theory works like this: it assumes that even as the church historically has passed down a particular theological position that is supposed to reveal what the Word of God says, there is quite often either a sacralization or a secularization in that hermeneutic. In other words, there are times a given passage or principle in the Word is "made holy" in order to benefit the ones doing the interpreting and to the deficit of the ones who are the targets of it. (That should be a wake-up call to Christians who don't spend much time reading the Bible.)

This flipside is secularization. To paraphrase Dr. Felder's theory, this means you water down the text, you bend it, you twist it, you distort or minimize what it says for your own benefit. Dr. Felder would acknowledge that this hermeneutical manipulation is not always conscious or even intentional. It is more often the result and consequences of the mindset of the culture in which the interpretation and utilization of the text is produced.

One of the strategies of marginalization is deceit. An authority is first established, and that authority dictates the position and behavior of its subjects. For instance, those who fled Europe in the name of religious freedom used that very freedom to religiously, philosophically and sociologically enslave other human beings, primarily human beings of color. This type of deception is one of the weapons in the arsenal of the enemy. The basic motive and method of deception is to make right seem wrong and wrong seem right. It is a deception that says, "It's alright for me to do this because Dr. So-And-So teaches that the Bible says it is."

The amazing historical observation is that an entire nation believed slavery was okay. They institutionalized it. Voted for it. Legislated it. And for the most part, they thought it was *right*. More than that, they believed it was the will of God. They had prayer meetings on it. They preached about it. They believed they were walking in and doing the very divine will of God.

The blending of an institutionalized ideology and an idealized theology gave birth to racism. I suggest that racism is a historical synthesis of an ideology and a theology. This blending would become the soil into which was planted the seeds of our Western democracy. The accepted deception was that the roots of a nation found their source in the godhead and was a revelation of divine will. An ideology. A theology. I want to take a closer look at each. I'll start with the ideology of racism, and then we will examine very closely, the erroneous biblical hermeneutic of racism. In this investigation we'll discover the fallacy of divine sanction.

Dr. Cornel West investigated racist origins and discovered this transition from a non-racist medical designation to a racist tool that went on to become the foundation of racism:

"Racism seems to have its roots in the early encounter between civilizations of Europe, Africa and Asia, encounters which occurred long before the rise of modern capitalism. The very category of race —denoting primarily skin color —was first employed as a means of classifying human bodies by François Bernier, a French physician, in 1684. The first substantial racial division of humankind is found in the influential Natural System (1735) of the pre-eminent naturalist of the 18th century, Carolus Linnaeus. Yet both instances reveal racist practices —in that both degrade and devalue non-Europeans —at the level of intellectual codification. Xenophontic folktales and mythologies, racist legends and stories —such as authoritative Church Fathers' commentaries on the Song of Solomon and the Ywain narratives in medieval Brittany —operate in the everyday lives of ordinary folk long before the 17th and 18th century. In fact, Christian anti-Semitism and European anti-blackish are rampant throughout the Middle Ages."[36]

---

36   West, Cornel. *Verso*, 22 March 2016. Article: "Race and Social Theory: Toward a Genealogical Materialist Analysis."

On the other side of the issue, "whiteness" is actually a social construct, a social commentary, and it goes as far back as the 14th century. Nobody was called white until then, yet it would become a politicized term that would be used as a distinction of hierarchy and privilege. Thus, the term designating the skin color assignment of "whiteness" was created in relationship to power and hierarchy over any other group so that increasingly throughout tradition and history the idea of whiteness rose as the principal priority of mankind in terms of status, socioeconomic access, political power, and economic resources.

"White is right" became the trend, the motto, and the rule of history.

"It's important to note that dating back to the first millennium AD, Africans existed in Europe, and, from about 711 AD to 1492 most of Spain was under Moorish control. Consequently, the Spanish colonizers who ventured forth to 'settle' lands outside of Europe did so while harboring color prejudice associated with their subjugation. But racial categories as we now know them, had not yet been used to justify the denial of basic rights, which were controlled through the church. By contrast, Europeans knew Africa to be a wealthy, advanced continent in many areas of development and education. When the American colonizers started the Atlantic slave trade, they weren't simply grabbing people out of the trees, as many of us were led to believe. They were targeting well established kingdoms weakened by internal strife, with citizens who had the skills required to develop the colonial enterprises, including advanced agricultural practices, metallurgy, navigation and shipbuilding, as well as the resources from the lands themselves. Race didn't begin to take on its modern meanings until the mid-16th century, and the terms and meanings that we now give to race in the U.S. weren't concretized until the early 20th century."[37]

37 Cruz, Anjana; in an article titled "Europeans invented the concept of race as we know it: Its origins can be traced to the colonization of the Americas"; July 21, 2017. See: https://timeline.com/europeans-invented-the-concept-of-race-as-we-know-it-58f896fae625

In the biblical world, as you proceed from Genesis through Revelation, there is virtually no hint of color prejudice. And where color is referred to in any negative way, it is a secondary, not primary, consideration. For example, God told His people not to intermarry, but not because whites or Semites shouldn't marry blacks; it was always for *spiritual* reasons—for purposes of the purity of one's religion. God told Solomon not to mess with the women over there, because they would lure him to serve their gods. It never mattered what color the women were; that was incidental. What mattered was spiritual purity.

Dr. Cain Hope Felder states, "Quite unlike today, the biblical world was essentially without color prejudice. Systematic treatments of 'race' or exotic theories of racism were alien to the ancient biblical authors who knew of the greatness of ancient African blacks and their glorious cultures, as reflected throughout the Bible."[38] Likewise, in the Scriptures there's no such thing as racism and black and color prejudice. It's important to understand that from Genesis through Revelation it's nowhere to be found.

The Genesis passage about Noah after the flood set the stage for all the earth being filled to the glory of God by the people of God out of one family. The emphasis is not on color; it's on the whole earth being filled. There's only one family left on the entire earth, and God ordains that earth be filled with glory, which means it can only be filled with glory if there are people in every part of the earth who declare His glory, which in turn means how the earth will be populated: with people who will glorify God. And those people were to come from the only eight people left on planet Earth after the Great Flood: Noah, his wife, his three sons and their wives.

How, then, has this come to mean that black people are cursed? It all depends on who's doing the interpreting of Scripture. It is not

---

38  Cain Hope Felder, *The Road We Trod* (Kindle Locations 237-238). Kindle Edition.

just what it says; it's what whoever says it says, what it really means, and who's actually doing what it means or acting on their own interpretation of it.

The concept of whiteness taking priority and being more authoritative has led to a serious form of racism—more, even, than color racism. Jarvis Williams and Kevin Jones introduced the idea of intellectual racism in their critique of the Southern Baptist Convention when they stated, "Intellectual racism is present in both Baptist schools and churches. Black and brown scholarship is either dismissed or ignored in many colleges, universities, and seminaries [which] have an overwhelming number of white leaders but few, if any black and brown leaders. Few Southern Baptist churches have multiethnic or minority leaders."[39] Williams and Jones then suggested this:

"White supremacy had its racist fangs in the ideology of American culture from this country's beginning....Thomas Jefferson, one of America's founding fathers, believed blacks were naturally inferior to whites. In his *Notes on the State of Virginia,* Jefferson stated, 'I advance it therefore as a suspicion only, that the blacks, whether originally a distinct race, or made distinct by time and circumstances, are inferior to the whites in the endowments both of body and mind' (Jefferson, Notes on the State of Virginia, 138-43). To be fair, Jefferson's notes state only that this was his 'suspicion.' Yet Jefferson is the same man who signed the Declaration of Independence, which affirmed 'all men are created equal.'"[40]

When one uses the cliché, "It's right there in black and white," as evidence of their position, they would do well to ask, "But who wrote the black and who wrote the white?" It's an extremely crucial distinction to make because *intellectual racism guards the gates of*

39    Williams, Jarvis J., Jones, Jr., Kevin M. *Removing the Stain of Racism from the Southern Baptist Convention.* Nashville: B&H Academic. 2017. Location 1027 of 3574. Kindle Edition
40    Ibid. Location 1052 of 3574

*the dissemination of intellectual property.* Intellectual racism is the gatekeeper. And intellectual racism is the first cousin to *institutional* racism (more likely, the *father* of institutional racism).

So always ask yourself, *Who wrote this book?* And be careful not to fall into the trap of thinking that just because it's written in a book, it must be true. The interpretation of the book will almost always be written from the perspective of, and filtered through, the *intellectual baggage of the writer.*

Fact is, however, you never know the whole story until you hear both sides. Intellectual dissemination of information has always been from the top down. If one group is on the top, then everything that comes forth from that culture will come from its perspective; in the case of racism and ethnic separation and division, this will be the "leading" intellectuals and theologians and politicians and anyone else on top with a point to make or an axe to grind. (And I promise you that those who are on top will never see it from the perspective of those who are on the bottom.)

You never get the whole story until you get the top and the bottom; just like you'll never get the bottom to speak if the top locks them out of the discourse. It is urgent that we learn to allow ourselves and others to hear the voices from below. That's why we must teach our children they have a voice and they have a word, a perspective. They must be given that privilege of knowledge. They must learn that they can speak out because the story will always be different if it's told from the bottom up. So, if the top says it is what it is, then it is—until you find out what the bottom has to say about it.

Echoing the earlier theory, Cornel West, Williams and Jones posit:

> "The English term race referenced human beings as a term
> of classification in the sixteenth century. In the eighteenth
> century, the term race was broadly applied to the diverse

populations of Native Americans, Africans, and Europeans in England's American colonies. In this historical context the term race developed to reference a hierarchal ranking system, which reflected English attitudes toward diverse groups of people. Conquered Indians were segregated from Europeans and exploited or expelled from their lands. The enslavement of Africans and their offspring was institutionalized in the late seventeenth and early eighteenth centuries. By then many Africans were identified as property."[41]

It's interesting that the clarion call from many quarters that there is no more racism in our culture today is coming from the top. I haven't heard many people from the other side, the bottom, the margin, the fringes, say anything like that. As the priority of a system in charge often tends to be to silence those who are at the bottom, we must consider the voices from the bottom because they have the rest of the story.

So now we see a definition of "racism" emerging: that which is the perspective of those who take a posture of priority and value and authority above or over those who are below.

As I mentioned, I was 30 years old before I ever knew that there were any black people in the Bible. I had gone to church all my life. When I was a little boy, going to Sunday school, we would be given a little card on which was printed the topic of the lesson for that day. One day, the lesson was "Suffer little children to come unto me." So, they gave us this card to take home to show our mother that we went to Sunday school instead of hanging out at Margulies, the local grocery store on the corner.

When I got home after church, I gave this little card to my mother, and it had a picture of a white Jesus on it. White Jesus was sitting on a rock, and He had a little white boy sitting on one knee

---

41  Ibid.

and a little white girl on the other knee, and there were little white kids sitting all around, looking up at Jesus. In the background of that depiction, outside of the circle of kids, was one lone little black kid.

I have never forgotten that card, because of all those little white kids clamoring around Jesus, sitting on the Lord's knee and there, in the back, shunted off to a corner, outside the little children coming unto Jesus, was one little black boy for our "Suffer the little children to come unto me" lesson. They may as well have tagged a line onto the lesson title reading, "except for the little black kid." How do you think that message affected a little black kid faithfully going to church every Sunday and being given a not-so-subtle message that Christianity might tolerate black but doesn't embrace black?

If the story is told from the top, it will always favor the perspective of those at the top. And as I look around in America today, black is not on top. Nowhere near. And it's nearly the year 2020.

One of the key ways that intellectual information was passed along in days gone by was not so much in books and writing but through art. I teach every summer at Oxford University in England, and my wife and I were touring there one summer and, as was my custom, we visited churches. We went from church to church and cathedral to cathedral. Some of these churches were built in the 500s and 600s. There are churches in England that are far older than America. Buildings and churches and cathedrals on the Oxford campus are older than the USA. When you go inside these old religious monuments, there are beautiful, elaborate mosaic windows made of stained glass. The pictures are just beautiful. Each scene depicted is in a specific sequence, so you can walk from one to the next and they tell an entire story. Sometimes they have the story of the 12 disciples. Sometimes they have the story of crossing the Red Sea. But they all teach the Bible through art because most of society could not read back when their churches were built. And this way, in church, though you might not be able to read the Bible, you can always see it depicted around you.

So, art becomes a didactic tool, the educator, the theologian in the Middle Ages and the dark ages. Art was one of the ways people learned. It was the "eye gate" through which information was received.

Art tells us the history of slavery. The first picture of the sons and descendants of Cush, the black people, were found on the walls of catacombs in caves hundreds of years before Christ. This was one way we could gain insight theologically, by looking at the paintings and depictions on the walls in caves. When we look at the art on these walls, it's interesting to see how people were depicted. Again, Egypt, Cush, Ethiopia, are all people of color, all descendants of Ham. We know that because some of the pictures and the drawings in these caves that are hundreds of years old depicted Egyptians for example. One of Ham's sons was Egypt, which means "dark" or burned. And in these caves and catacombs and other places, drawings depict Egyptians in dark statues and sculptures, dark in pictures on walls and in caves. These people were Egyptians. Hundreds, even thousands, of years before Christ, Egyptians were depicted with dark skin.

Fast forward to Matthew chapter 2, verse 13: "When they had gone, an angel of the Lord appeared to Joseph in a dream and said, 'Get up. Take the child and His mother and escape to Egypt.'" Take the child Jesus to Egypt. So, think it through: the goal was to hide the child. Get Him away from the murderous Herod. Get Him over to Egypt. But if the Christ child had white skin, blond hair and blue eyes, as depicted in many churches and assumed by many people, how were they going to hide Him among all that Egyptian chocolate in the land of dark-skinned people? Don't you think somebody in the neighborhood might have noticed and phoned in the little odd-looking white Jewish kid with blond hair and blue eyes trying to hide? Doesn't take a genius to figure out that you can't hide a blonde-haired, blue-eyed baby in what we just established has been for hundreds of years a black culture and black context.

In the oldest depictions and drawings of Jesus, He is seen as a man with black skin. In fact, those earliest depictions of Him give Him a hair style that looks a little like the Afro I used to wear. Now, I understand that logic will frighten some people at the top of white Christian enterprises or in Caucasian families today, but you can't fake that kind of news. Cush is a land of black faces. Egypt is a land of black. Certainly, these terms do not imply whiteness. So, if the smartest place to hide the infant Jesus was in Egypt, where He could blend in with other kids, it's only logical they did it because they knew he'd blend in among the people.

A Google search result on the oldest known depiction of Jesus states that it was, "found in Syria and dated to about 235, shows Him as a beardless young man of authoritative and dignified bearing. He is depicted dressed in the style of a young philosopher, with close-cropped hair and wearing a tunic and pallium—signs of good breeding in Greco-Roman society."[42] And that was more than 200 years after Jesus ascended to Heaven. I doubt somebody drew Him from memory. But at least it was in Syria and offered a description without delineating skin color, allowing the assumption that the subject was at least Semitic.

It was not until the sixth century that we see the first and the oldest portrait of Jesus as a white man. Still, let's settle this right now: nobody knows what Jesus looks like, because nobody who saw Him is still alive to tell you what He looked like. And more often than not, an artist would choose a friend or even a stranger as the model for religious portraits. So, the dark-skinned Jesus in the first portrait from the third century is then depicted a few hundred years later as a white man. How did that happen?

---

42  See Google search: https://www.google.com/
    url?sa=i&source=images&cd=&ved=2ahUKEwjH0viEv__

In the fourth century (in the 380s), everything changed when a man, a Roman ruler, by the name of Constantine got saved and, in what he assumed was a very spiritual thing, declared that the entire Roman world should be Christian. That set the stage a few years after Constantine died, for a guy to decree that the legal and official religion of the Roman Empire was Christianity—despite all the idol gods and all the nations around them that served idol gods.

Constantine and the political authorities of the Roman empire were European. Christianity being elevated to the status of *the* religion of the Roman Empire gave rise to art. And artists create in their own image as they see through their own eyes and perspective. Starting around the year 300 AD, the big dog in the world was the Roman Empire, so the portrait of Jesus from the sixth century was the product of artists who painted the image for those who were in control. The Europeans. More precisely, the *Western* Europeans. The lighter-skinned ones. And *viola*—white Jesus. Which makes sense politically and artistically, because it depicts the view from the top echelons. Now we have hundreds of years of Jesus produced by the dominant culture and depicted with blonde or auburn hair, blue or auburn eyes, and white skin.

But the baby Jesus hid in Egypt for the first five years of His life, so somewhere between then and now comes forth a Jesus who could hail from a southern rock band.

A voice from the group at the top might retort, "So what? What difference does it make? Why are you spending all this time on this? What does it matter if we depict our Lord as looking more like us? God is a spirit. They who worship Him must worship Him in spirit and in truth. Doesn't really matter what color Jesus was."

But we're not talking about the spirit of Jesus. We're discussing the physical flesh and blood of Jesus. If He was born and walked the streets of Jerusalem, He looked like something. And it's okay to depict Him as He mostly likely appeared, for the sake of honesty if for no other reason.

One night a little girl was crying and having bad dreams.

Her daddy said, "Don't cry. Jesus is with you. Jesus is with you."

He went back to sleep and a couple of minutes later, he heard, "Daddy, Daddy, Daddy, Daddy."

He went back to her bedroom and said again, "Don't cry. Jesus is with you. Go back to sleep."

"But, Daddy," the little girl said, "I need somebody with skin."

I'm always intrigued when I hear about people who say they "saw" Jesus in a vision or a dream. I always want to ask them what color His eyes and skin are. Or when people say, "Jesus told me," I always want to ask if He had a deep voice or a high voice. I don't mean to come across as cynical or incredulous, but I've always wondered how He looked and sounded. Most people probably wonder about that. Why wouldn't we? He's our Savior.

Another point of interest is that racism always includes an economic dynamic. If you go to Egypt, you go to the pyramids. All that labor was done by somebody. And, trust me, it didn't include too many people from the top of society.

The key about slavery is that it included people of many different hues and shades and colors. Not all slaves were black. In his book *All You Need to Know*, James Walvin wrote, "Most of the most famous structures from lost civilizations were built by slaves. Today, swarms of tourists visit the Pyramids in Egypt, and those in meso-America, not to mention the more recent architectural splendors of classical Greece and Rome. All were the work of slaves... But most slaves to be found in classical Greece and Rome were white—not black." [43]

The Civil War was not just political. It was just as much economic. The whole industrial foundation of the South was dependent and built upon the backs of slaves. The White House was built by slaves.

---

43  Walvin, James. *All You Need to Know...Slavery: The History and Legacy of One of The World's Most Brutal Institutions*. Malta: Connell Publishing (2018; p. 7, 10).

The authors of all those documents and declarations and constitutions were all slave owners. A U.S. President or two is known to have fathered children with his black slaves. Hence, even the government is in the mix on the issue of slavery. Jeremy Black reflected on this idea in his work, *Slavery: A New Global History*:

> "In the case of the New World, slaving indeed served to build up a labor force based on fungible human collateral for the credit that supported an Atlantic trading system that grew through very heavy borrowing from Europe. This, however, is far too narrow an account of slavery, for it omits totally the significance of public slavery: slavery in the service of the state, which is a key strand from antiquity to the present. ...Slavery, therefore, is a state with different meanings in particular contexts, but with a fundamental element of an absence of freedom....Indeed, far from seeing sale, purchase and sellability as key elements of slavery, they were, and are, particular means of exchange within one of the two central forms of slave society, with governmental power providing the other element. Moreover, the classic Atlantic slave trade depended on both capitalist exchange and government power, as African polities produced slaves through warfare, just as polities for much of history supported slave markets by these means."[44]

So, the curse of Ham became the theo-philosophical core of justification and legitimization of the institution of slavery in America. The Genesis 9 passage became the core, the legitimization, the authoritative foundation that the entire system of slavery in America was built on. America got it from Europe. And in the crossings of the Atlantic related to the slave trade, it brought with it

---

44   Black, Jeremy. *Slavery: A New Global History*. Philadelphia: Running Press (2011; p. 10-11).

a top mindset, based on that one passage and its misinterpretation. A misinterpretation that said that God said black people are cursed. When God never said that. A misinterpretation that says God said you will serve and be servants. When God never said that. Yet, they say God said it, and they point to the passage in Genesis to "prove" it (albeit falsely).

You have never been in a fight until you get into a fight with somebody convinced God is on their side. This idea of God-ordained racism appeared in the dastardly demonic blight known as apartheid in the country of South Africa. Apartheid was an ungodly, complicated blanket of racism woven into the fabric of a nation with threads of theological error based primarily on the belief that God told us to do it.

A dear pastor friend of mine stood in line for eight hours to vote in the first election of Dr. Nelson Mandela for President of South Africa. This act "began" the process of dismantling apartheid. My friend said it will take generations to rid the country of the complex system. In his book, *South Africa and the Powers Behind,* Derek Morphew states:

> "The frustrating fact is that apartheid is a massive, complex, interrelated web of laws, traditions, attitudes, socio-political, economic and theological factors. It is a system which cannot simply die in a week or even a year. It has to be unraveled and reversed with as much determination and patience as it was once woven into our society. This process can be accelerated or retarded, but it will never be simple because apartheid is not simple."[45]

Other than 9-1-1, I have visited South Africa almost every year since Dr. Mandela was released from Robben Island. It is a deeply

---

45  Morphew, Derek. *South Africa and the Powers Behind*. Derek Morphew Publishing. Kindle Edition. Location 1391 of 3076.

spiritual nation. It is a proud people. It is a resilient culture.

"South Africa is a very religious country," Derek Morphew writes. "Consequently, for most of our people theology lies behind ethics, ethics lies behind attitudes, and attitudes influence the political process. Further, from the biblical perspective such ideological structures have an invisible power factor which can only be dealt with in this arena. That is why the philosophical and theological roots of apartheid have to be thoroughly dealt with."[46]

Notwithstanding the fact that no one could "settle" or even "discover" a land that is already settled by its own inhabitants, Dutch "settlers" of South Africa came with a warped European theology, as Morphew notes:

> "The early settlers landed at the Cape. The first settlement was founded by the Dutch but later annexed by the British. This created a situation where predominantly Dutch settlers were living under British administration. Tensions were bound to arise.... If one looks a little closer, one discovers economic and language factors as well. Included in these factors one finds the issue of race. This was interwoven with the Dutch/English tension because the British administration followed a racial policy which the Dutch farmers resented."[47]

The only slightly more spiritual British abolished slavery in 1833, which sparked rebellion in 1834 by the Dutch farmers. However, closer examination of what appears to be such a noble political gesture reveals that there was a fundamental theological element in this legislation. One of the Dutch scribes explained the mindset of the Dutch in light of the abolishment of slavery, stating that the freedom of the slaves represented a "shameful

---

46  Ibid.
47  Ibid. Location 1412 of 3076.

and unjust proceeding" and stated, "Yet it is not their freedom that drove us to such lengths, as their being placed on an equal footing with Christians, contrary to the laws of God and of the natural distinction of race and religion, so that it was intolerable for any decent Christian to bow beneath such a yoke, wherefore we withdrew in order to preserve our doctrines of purity."[48]

Derek Morphew notes that behind this declaration was the assumption that anyone who was not European could not be equal with a Christian, exposing the chilling belief that *only Europeans could be Christians,* and all others were by definition inferior. "The distinction of "race" is equated with the distinction of "religion,"" Morphew writes. Notice also that from the very beginning such assumptions have a theological base. There are Christian "doctrines of purity" to be maintained. "While economic, political, and language (English) factors were also involved, the race issue is obvious."[49]

There developed a battle between biblical theology and what I call political theology. The abolishment of slavery would have an impact on the practice of theology. As one example, if a non-European was now seen as "equal" under the law, was he also equal under church law? The admittance of non-Europeans into the fold of Christianity would require admittance to the ordinances of the church. In other words, whoever "accepted Christianity" must be accepted into the life of the Christian church, with all the rights and privileges of the church (as they used to say in the Baptist church where I grew up), such as baptism, the Lord's Table, church membership, and so forth. This was to be done in accordance with the Scriptures on the authority of the revealed word of God. This was not to be tolerated by the grassroots members of the church. The position of the biblically literate would be overruled by the growing voices of dissent and rejection.

It reminds me of a now-deceased deacon at the church I

---

48  Ibid. Location 1422 of 3076.
49  Ibid.

pastor. In the context of my teaching on the biblical principles of church discipline (referring to the practical action called forth in Matthew 18:17, "Let him be to you like a heathen and tax collector"—that is, dismiss him from the fellowship), this deacon declared to me, "Preacher, I don't care what this Bible says, I'm not gonna do it." The deacon then left the church. Those were the last words I ever heard from him. A few months later, while watching college football on a Saturday afternoon, he asked his wife to get him a beverage from the kitchen. When she returned, she discovered that he had dropped dead in his chair.

That's essentially what the Boer/Dutch "Christians" said. *We don't care what the Bible says, we will not accept indigenous South Africans as equals.* In response to the resistance of the grassroots constituency of the Dutch Reformed Church, the leadership met in 1857 and passed the following statement:

> "The Synod considers it to be desirable and in accordance with Scripture that our converts from paganism be received and incorporated into existing congregations, wherever possible; however, where this practice, because of the weakness of some, constitutes an obstacle to the advancement of Christ's cause among pagans, congregations formed or still to be formed from converts from paganism should be given the opportunity to enjoy their Christian privileges in a separate place of worship"[50] (de Gruchy & Villa-Vicencio, page 19).

Phrases like "because of the weakness of some" and converts be given the "opportunity to enjoy Christian privileges in a separate place" are buzz phrases for the sociological oxymoron "separate but equal," and eerily harken to American slavery language.

---

50   Ibid. Location 1445 of 3076

Morphew writes, "In 1881 this 'weakness' became a missionary policy and a separate church was formed for reaching the 'coloured' people. This date should be taken as the official origin of apartheid as a social structure. This is why apartheid is first and foremost a church issue. The political structure was to follow much later."[51]

The foundation of apartheid was a eisegetical hermeneutic of South African ecclesiology, which would be seen by the ruling masses as theological justification, validation, and authority for keeping non-Europeans in their "God-given" place—at the bottom of the society. This false theology limited the evangelistic gospel mandate of Matthew 28 to their own kind. The assignment to reach "all nations" did not and would not include other races, but only non-Jewish Gentiles. All nations ("panta ta ethne") did not imply other races, but other non-Jewish members of the Roman Empire. Morphew cites the following summary:

> "Apartheid was now actively proposed by the church as a biblical, ethical policy with positive value. The 'weakness' of some became the 'biblical' policy of the church and the advice given by the church to the state.... As a Church, we have always worked purposefully for the separation of the races. In this regard apartheid can rightfully be called a Church policy."[52]

Wow. Stunning. Open promotion of racism as Church *policy*. The system of apartheid could be seen as the South African version of American slavery. Both of them relegated people of color to the domain of the dregs of society. Both would use the Bible as the authority for their theo-sociological constructs. In effect, the slave master would establish God as authority and His word as the revelation of His will. This put the Bible and even the church itself

---

51   Ibid. Location 1449 of 3076
52   Ibid. Location 1471 of 3076

into a position of an overseer's whip as a method of keeping the "darkies" in their place.

But then, something unexpected and uncontrollable evolved, and everything changed when black folk found a Bible. With the Bible and often the church itself as tools of control over the institution of slavery, the American church has been leading the front of racism, racist institutions, and the perpetuation of bias and prejudice in the fabric of this country. By the front, I mean because of the mantra "God told us to," with regard to slavery. Slavery, in other words, was explained by the church as *an act of obedience to God*.

Once the slaves found the Bible, they began to realize it was being used as a weapon and tool for control over them through the preaching coming from both white preachers and black preachers who preached what the White preachers told them to preach. Slaves heard the Word, but they heard it from these two sources. When the slaves illegally began studying the Bible for themselves, things began to shift.

I'm not a prophet nor the son of the prophet, but I declare this unto you: Black Christians are one of the greatest miracles of modern history, because the very thing that the enemy meant for evil, God turned it around for Kingdom good. And the equipment that was used to enslave us became the very tool for liberty to get us out and to get us through.

Possibly the most famous example of this was the slave preacher Nat Turner. Things were about to change when Turner learned to read. He read Ephesians 6:5, the favorite passage of the slave master and white preacher: "Slaves obey your masters." But what they didn't realize was that Nat got his own copy of the Bible and turned the page from Ephesians 6 to read, "Be strong in the Lord and in the power of His might," and, "take up the whole armor of God, that you may be able to withstand in the evil day.

And having done all, to stand." And Nat kept turning the pages to other books in his Bible and found, "Stand...and take the sword of the Spirit, which is the Word of God." He kept turning and found, "For me to live is Christ, and to die is gain." He kept turning pages and read, "That I may know Him and the power of His resurrection. He turned some more and found, "If God is for us, who can be against us?" He found, "We are more than conquerors through Him who loved us." (Ephesians 6:10,14; Philippians 1:21; 3:10; Romans 8:31, 37)

They should have snatched that Bible out of Nat's hand because when Nat got hold of that Bible all hell was about to break loose as he read where Moses warned Pharaoh: "Let my people go!" If God delivered Daniel, why could He not deliver Nat?

He saw walls coming down when Joshua fought the battle of Jericho. He saw the chains and shackles of bondage being cut away. He read about three Hebrew boys in the fiery furnace, and God walked them out of it.

Black Christians are the greatest miracle of modern history because no other people was systematically, authoritatively and legitimately shut out of the grace of God and the truth of God, yet as a people they learned to walk by faith and not by sight. Once God got in the middle of the slave camps and the slave shacks, and once God found some Nat Turners and other folk who were willing to keep standing on the Bible, the whole Kingdom of God was opened to them. The slaves may have been shut out and shackled in a system of systematic, institutionalized degradation, but when God got His hand in it, what the devil meant for evil, God turned around for good.

You must have some "But God" spaces in your life where the only way you got through it was that where the enemy had laid the trap (often even using Christians to lay it), God stepped in and abolished the trap. The more you look at it, the more you see the hand of God. God has had His hand on American people of color. We will never back down from that. To God be the glory.

African Americans have a historical testimony. We kept turning Bible pages long enough to realize that in God there is no Jew, no Gentile, no top, no bottom, no haves and no have-nots. We are all one family from one blood, not by accident. It was God's plan from the very beginning. So, we can't look down. We can't let our children look down. We can't let this next generation keep looking down at their iPhones and iPads so much that they miss what God has to say.

One of my favorite movies is the story surrounding a slave ship called the *Amistad*. The passengers were brought to America in chains as slaves. These slaves could not speak English and certainly could not read. They barely understood. A part of their challenge of being slaves in America was they had to learn how to piecemeal messages. But one slave got hold of a Bible, and it had pictures in it, and this scene in the movie showed slaves learning about Jesus through the pictures. The sequence of the panels told the story of Jesus, and they saw how He suffered, how He was dragged before Pilate on trumped up charges, and they learned just by reading the pictures how the system was perverted and twisted against them. Page after page drew them closer and closer to the story of Jesus. They couldn't read a word of it, but looking at the pictures led them to the power of God. Reading the pictures built their faith in Jesus.

Don't ever box God in. God will get His Word to you one way or another. He's bigger than any box. He didn't make a mistake when He made you. Your color, your ethnicity, your journey, are all part of your story. Your story is a demonstration of this great God who loves you with an everlasting love. Your story is a story of His great power.

Racism in black and white (or any other hue) is nullified by God's own word. Paul puts it this way in Galatians 3:28: "There is neither Jew nor Greek, slave nor free, male nor female, for you are all one in Christ Jesus." Hymnist Annie Flint put it this way in the song "He Giveth More Grace":

> *His love has no limits, His grace has no measure,*
> *His power no boundary known unto men;*
> *For out of His infinite riches in Jesus*
> *He giveth, and giveth, and giveth again.*[53]

53   "He Giveth More Grace," Annie J. Flint. Copyright in Public Domain.

# 4

# THE HALLOWED HALLS OF HYPOCRISY

*"The hypocrite's crime is that he bears false witness against himself.*
*What makes it so plausible to assume that hypocrisy is the*
*vice of vices is that integrity can indeed exist under the cover*
*of all other vices except this one. Only crime and the criminal,*
*it is true, confront us with the perplexity of radical evil; but only the*
*hypocrite is really rotten to the core."*
**—Hannah Arendt,** *On Revolution*[54]

*The cop swung his truncheon hard and hit a girl in the stomach*
*with such force that the blow lifted her clean off the floor and knocked*
*her over the back of one of the ornate couches that adorned the*
*normally quiet study space in the Union lobby.*

*In a matter of minutes, the building was surrounded. Police*
*blocked every entrance. My girlfriend and I had no idea what was going*
*on as we clung to each other, shaking in fright while we were roughly*
*herded forward with scores of other black faces by a squad of "law*
*enforcement" officers from the back of the building toward the front*
*entrance and who knows what awaited us...*

\* \* \*

I have taught on the college level at several institutions of
higher learning. My ultimate goal as a teacher is to help my students
learn to think. I am inspired by the revelation of the spiritual life
of the Bereans and of the biblical exhortation "Come, let us reason

---

54    Arendt, Hannah (1906-1975), *On Revolution* (Ch. 2).

together." The prophet Isaiah raises this proposition in the context of a sinful Israel before a holy God. His invitation to participate in the process of reason is related to Israel's undeniable sinfulness, but the challenge is to engage in a judicial process of validity assessment.

Isaiah creates a spiritual court where the people of God are on trial for their sinful rejection of their covenant God. Isaiah creatively speaks of the scene as a covenant lawsuit—God is taking them to court. The prophet describes the process as "debating the case in court."[55] As the *Theological Wordbook of the Old Testament* states it, "This judicial element (which is the primary meaning of *yakaw*) has a clear theological basis as seen in Isaiah 11:3, where the activities of 'the Stem of Jesse, the Branch' is spoken of as one who 'will not judge...by what his eyes see, nor make a decision by what his ears hear.'"[56]

When one of my mentors, the late Dr. E. K. Bailey, taught me a principle of biblical interpretation, he warned against being guilty of "credulity," which he defined as "belief without investigation." Similar to the "hermeneutic of suspicion" principle of interpretation he taught me to question the source and validity of a truth. These two guidelines lead to fundamental questions like: "Who said that?" and "Who passed that on?" The goal is to discover how much variation there was between the source and the intermediary sources.

I must confess, as I look back over my academic journey, I have been guilty of theological credulity and often failed to exercise the hermeneutic of suspicion. I took some things at their word without deeper investigation. I have, in my files and archives, notes from classes and sermons that I have delivered over the years that show where I had learned and then staunchly taught and preached against the modern day practice of spiritual gifts.

---

55  *Theological Wordbook of the Old Testament.* © 1980 by The Moody Bible Institute of Chicago. All rights reserved. Used by permission.
56  Ibid.

I remember being in a class where my significantly conservative, not-at-all empathic to charismatics and Pentecostals, professor danced around the edges of stating that all Pentecostals and charismatics were going to hell. Needless to say, the trajectory of my own spiritual journey and the content and emphasis of my personal spiritual life and teaching and preaching ministry shifted when I personally experienced what is referred to as the "baptism of the Holy Spirit." My point is that the theological shift came about when I finally exercised a hermeneutic of suspicion and refused to take comfort or exercise credulity in the didactic influence of those with the power to give me a pass or fail grade. Truth over ego.

I must confess that I went through a period of spiritual depression and even anger over the fact that I had swallowed someone else's opinion—hook line and sinker—with all of the cultural experiential baggage that they brought with them to the text. I often wondered and suspected that my theological positions would be different had I attended a more liberal scholastic academy.

Maybe the most difficult realization has been the suspicion of deliberate academic hypocrisy in which opposing positions were not only rejected and ignored but maybe even deliberately extracted from the curricula. I have "found" material which at best challenges popular scholarly positions and may even contradict the academic status quo. I suspect some dwellers of the intellectual high towers have looked down on certain "discoveries" and "revelations" that go contrary to the party line and arrogantly dismissed them or at least discredited them because they didn't line up with the long line of establishment positions.

I don't see this as a shade of racism as much as it is indicative of the mentality of the gatekeepers of knowledge, who I believe in many cases vet ideas not on their intrinsic value and potential contribution to the discussion, but to the degree that such ideas reinforce and validate what has already been positioned as the pinnacle of knowledge and wisdom in theological academia. They seem to have come to a point in their internal spiritual knowledge comfort level where they no longer (if they ever did at all) investigate, study, question, or think accepted dogma through. They don't want to rock the boat. They simply accept what others told them earlier. Curiosity is indeed the mother of discovery.

The introduction of opposing truths is akin to the challenge faced by biblical ambassadors of Kingdom truths in a society intellectually controlled by opposing sects of Scribes and Pharisees, which the early disciples faced. The community of the academy is not about money. It is not even about fame, per se. It's about *power*. It is about intellectual power and the control of it. I think this proposition is especially true in the hallowed halls of the theological academy. I get it that we are to contend for the truth. I stand on and commit my life to the exhortation of Jude 3-4: "Dear friends, although I was very eager to write to you about the salvation we share, I felt I had to write and urge you to contend for the faith that was once for all entrusted to the saints." The truth of the Lord is worth fighting for!

However, I find that the greater challenge is the area of historical, cultural and extra-biblical findings that influence the interpretation of those timeless truths. This goes contrary to the invitation to "reason together." It's as if opposing views are convicted without trial, debate, or discussion. I acknowledge that this is one man's position, based on one man's intellectual journey. But to a student of Scripture, who was almost 30 years old at the time, having been raised in church all my life (including accepting Christ as my Lord and Savior at the age of ten), I learned that most academies are structured and strive to present their truth as ex cathedra, infallible, and not to be questioned (at least where I studied). I understood that from an intellectual perspective, but when I put myself back in the seat of the student, I realize that the quest for theological purity has often compromised objectivity and legitimacy, and the student is most often left in the position of the great granddaughter who eventually questioned the family method of baking a Christmas ham.

As it often occurs, this parable has had many iterations and variations. Was it ham? Turkey? Pot roast? I think I have heard each version over the years. But actually, I suggest these details are inconsequential to the conclusion and application of the revelation that comes forth from the story. This version with fictitious names goes something like this:

This extended family has...an excellent tradition. On the second Saturday in December, they have a...traditional feast in their family households. On that day, they all prepare a delicious baked ham.

Gwen makes one, Helen makes one, Jacqueline does, and so does Katie. Even though it's really just Katie and her husband nowadays, she makes a small one anyway because she loves to participate in the family tradition.

And they all fix their hams in exactly the same way. They prepare a special glaze with brown sugar, raisins, some cloves, a hint of allspice, red pepper, and a half cup of whiskey. They put all those ingredients into a bowl and whisk them together, then warm the glaze on the stove.

Then they cut off the end of the ham, toss it out, place the remaining ham into the roaster pan and pour the glaze over it until it puddles just a bit underneath the ham. The ham is roasted at 350 degrees for 2 ½ hours, and its ready to eat.

Gwen and Ed were newlyweds last year and learning about each other's family traditions. So, Ed was in the kitchen helping Gwen prepare the ham and was watching as she cut the end of the ham off and threw it away.

Naturally he was curious about this and asked, "Gwen, why do you cut that part of the ham off and throw it away? It looks perfectly fit to eat."

Gwen replied, "I don't know. My mother always did it that way; so that's the way I do it."

Ed was unhappy with that answer because he thought it was just a waste of good food. So, he asked Gwen if she would please ask her mom why the ham has to have the end cut off before it goes into the oven.

Gwen finished up in the kitchen and rang her Mom up on the phone and asked, "Mom, why do you always cut the end of the ham off and throw it away before putting the ham into the oven?"

Helen replied, "Well, honey, I'm not really sure; that's the way my mom always did it, so I always do it that way too. And over the years I have thrown away a lot of ham ends. That just how it is. But you know what? I could call and ask your grandmother the reason."

After several more calls to find the "family secret," the girls learned that the *real* reason Grandma cut the end of the ham off and threw it away. The ham was too big for the cooking pot![57]

The entire topic of unquestioningly accepting what has been told to us by those in positions of "authority" or seniority or position, has challenged me with questions that often embarrass and even anger me, due to my naïveté. No more. I try to teach my students that one indication of academic maturity is to question the teacher!

I was raised in an African American Baptist Church that was pastored by a giant of a pastor (over 6'5"). Dr. W. B. Rouse was the

---

57   Shook, Michael. *The Legend Of The Ham Pan*. Plain spoken positive thinker. Learning to change habitual thoughts. November 8, 2017 https://thriveglobal.com/stories/the-legend-of-the-ham-pan/

first biblical scholar to touch my life. I think the seeds of my passion for the Word of God came from Him. (In fact, when he passed, he left me several of his books.) As I look back on it, I *never* heard one sermon, Sunday school lesson, or lecture on the presence of blacks in the Bible. Like the women with the ham, I just assumed what was taught was the way it was. I didn't question it. I just assumed there were no black people in the Bible.

Because I was a musician, I trafficked in and out of most of the black churches in the small town of East St. Louis, Illinois. I often saw, passed by, and never questioned the theology behind all black churches with pictures of a white Jesus either hanging in the church or portrayed in stained glass windows. This of course reinforced my erroneous conclusion that black people had no place in the biblical story. I did not let my lack of hermeneutic of suspicion dissuade me from my journey of credulity.

I think the first significant theological question I ever raised was related to skin color and the Bible. I had seen pictures and stained glass images of a white Jesus on the walls of black churches. I was so keenly aware of the segregation in the town I was raised in and the contrast of walking down neighborhood streets filled with people of color then venturing downtown and walking down Collinsville Avenue (the main drag in "downtown" E. St. Louis) and seeing white shoppers going in and out of stores run by white shop owners. It was not at all psychologically damaging to me (the result of solid parental upbringing). I was simply aware of the difference.

By the way, I once asked a question in a class I taught on racial reconciliation that sparked a long discussion among my mostly white students. I ask them how old they were when they realized they were white. There was a brief period of contemplative silence. One said he was ten years old and cited an incident in school involving a black kid. One was in junior high school. Some were in their teenaged years. Some couldn't remember. All of the black students said they had always known they were black. I lived down the street from a white-owned hardware store and a block from a Jewish-owned small grocery store. I have always known I was black.

So, when I went to church on Sundays and sat in my Sunday School classes, learning biblical stories about Bible characters and Bible verses, I would often wonder what their neighborhoods looked like. What side of town did they live in? What color were they? I was never told they were white. I just assumed they were because I saw the stained glass windows and the Sunday school topic cards. But these biblical characters were biblical heroes. They were biblical role models and spiritual blessings. They had to look like *something*. I was taught that God created man in His own image. God had to look like *something*.

The Bible says God created man out of the dust, the dirt, earth. In fact, by the time God created man, streams of water came up from the earth and watered the whole surface of the ground. And the Lord God formed the man of the ground and breathed into his nostrils the breath of life, and the man became a living being (Genesis 2:6-7). So, there was dirt mixed with water, which became clay. So, God made man out of clay. Which suggests care and intent in the making of man. But...clay is *brown*. Mud is even darker. What color was the mud that God used to make man?

My inquisitive scholastic mind started asking the obvious questions. Extended contemplation on my academic journey and the systems that have shaped me has often left me frustrated and sometimes angry. I became miffed (A better word would be *incensed*.) that no one had ever broached the topic with me. I was appalled that it wasn't important enough to my Bible teachers and pastors and professors to bring up the issue—until I acknowledged that my mind-shapers were of the dominant culture; then it began to make sense.

Yet, when I became the one standing at the front of the room, when I became the professor of record, when I became the one who stood before a congregation and said, "Turn with me...," I would often feel I was complicit in the deprivation of exposure to the crossroad of historical realities and biblical revelation. In other words, *truth*. Because, at its core, I was being fed some fake (or let's say "well massaged") parts of the Good News.

Words like *hypocrisy* and *conspiracy* raced through my mind and my heart. No one told me. I found a bit of consolation in the fact that we are all products and casualties of our environment, nurture, and influence of exposure. Still, the more I wrestled with it, the more depressing it got. It was very hard, personally. It has been hard professionally too, because I have been exposed to, and have come to realize, the hypocrisy that often characterizes the academic and scholastic intellectual circles in which I run.

*Hypocrisy* is a good word. I was trying to think of a better word, but that's a good one. The word *hypocrite* comes from a Greek word used in the theatre. The actor, with minimal costumes, would switch masks between one with a smile and one with frown to depict the shifting pathos of the script. Happy, sad; smile, frown. Jesus used the word hypocrite in Luke 6:42. It is the idea of masking the truth. For me, it was often masking the reality of my doubts. I learned how to dance around the obvious, implying its insignificance.

If God made man out of clay, held it in His hands and shaped the clay into a living man, it had to look like something. If Jesus walked the earth as a man, clothed in flesh and blood, His flesh had to have a color, a hue, a shade.

I believe someone "back there" knew better and knew more than they admitted. I believe this failure to disclose was based on the fear that some of their discoveries would destroy traditional myths that validated estrangement, exclusion, and devaluation of a people who had been marginalized. I think there has been a generation of scholars and investigators who feared repercussions from the hallowed halls of intellectual and academic power.

I experienced something similar when I went up to defend my Ph.D. dissertation at Grace Graduate School of Theology. The story takes a humbling twist at the end. The topic and title of my dissertation was "Theology in the Music of the Black Church in America as an Element of Church Growth." (You have to have a long title for these documents, so they can sound appropriately highfalutin', deep, and important!) In my project, I did a theological analysis of the lyrics of the music of the black church back to slavery. My thesis was a spin-off of the doctoral thesis of one of my mentors, Dr. Wyatt Tee Walker. Dr. Walker was one of the students in the first class of Dr. Martin Luther King, Jr., Fellows at Colgate Rochester/Bexley Hall/Crozer. His thesis explained that "what black people are singing religiously will provide a clue as to what is happening to them sociologically."[58] The thesis of my dissertation was a variation on Dr. Walker's work.

I posited that "if you want to know what black people believe, theologically, listen to what they sing musically." The document was a sort of systematic exposé on the theology embedded in the music of black culture that came forth from the dreaded slavery period of the United States. In my dissertation, I cite Walker's refutation of long-accepted views of African religion as polytheistic. Particularly, Walker challenges the "reports" of white European missionaries and explorers who declared that the black Africans were worshipers of trees and could be seen dancing and worshiping around the tree. Walker observes that the Westernized bias of Europeans who assumed that what they deemed to be tree worship was in fact a misinterpretation of African theology and worship. Walker wrote:

> "The monotheism of West African traditional religion provided fertile ground for the development of the 'invisible church.' ...We knew Him (the true and living God) as

---

58    Walker, Wyatt Tee. *Somebody's Calling My Name: Black Sacred Music and Social Change.* Valley Forge: Judson Press: pg. 17.

early as the fifth century A.D....[and] possessed a religious heritage founded on the one-God principle."[59]

Walker goes on to declare that the white missionaries and explorers who saw Africans dancing around the tree failed to discern that the festive activities around the tree was not worship of the tree but worship of the God who provided the tree....

" ...The Africans did not 'worship' the tree as a god, but as a container of the 'life' which God places in the tree to be a sustainer of the 'worshiper.' The African worshiper knew God had given life to the tree, and that if he picked the fruit of the tree, it would give him life. He knew God had given the tree life, and that the bark and wood of the tree could be used to build a hut, which would sustain his life. He knew God had given life to the tree, and if he cut the tree down, he could hollow out the trunk and make a canoe for travel and fishing. His 'worship' was not a deification of the tree, but an acknowledgment of God's material provision."[60]

My proctor told me I could not include this information in my final document. He said it smacks of animism, which, according to the *Dictionary of Theological Terms*, is "the belief that inanimate objects possess a soul or spirit or that they are indwelt by spirits. Often the indwelling spirit is thought to be that of the departed, resulting in ancestor worship. Animistic religion is a religion of fear. Some New Age advocates view animism as a way of deifying the earth."[61] I find it interesting that the work from which this quote is

---

59   Walker, Wyatt Tee, *The soul of Black Worship* (New York: Martin Luther King Fellows Press, 1984,) pp 10-11.

60   Ulmer, Kenneth. *Theology in the Music of the Black Church in America As An Element of Church Growth*. Unpublished dissertation. 1986.

61   Cairns, A. *Dictionary of Theological Terms*. Ambassador Emerald International; Greenville, SC. (2002; p. 28).

taken has a cross reference to this article that takes you to the heading
"See African Theology," where you find the following entry:

> "The attempt to marry the theology of traditional African
> religions with contemporary 'Christian' faith; 'an attempt
> to synthesize Christianity with African traditional
> religions' (Byang H. Kato, *Theological Pitfalls in Africa*, p.
> 55). African theology is not merely the interpretation of
> Christian theology by African theologians, using African
> thought forms. It is the exploration of what the traditional,
> pre-Christian, animistic religions have been saying on
> the presupposition that they represent authentic divine
> revelation. In the subsequent synthesis with Christianity
> the Bible's data are accepted only if they support what has
> already been established from the traditional religions. In
> itself, *the Bible is not the source of truth for proponents of
> African theology.*"[62] (Emphasis added)

Again, it is not the scope of *this* work to debate the validity
of Dr. Walker's position that African Theology was monotheistic
and morphed from monotheism to more traditional Christianity
via the introduction of Jesus Christ as Savior. Dr. Walker would
say the leap from monotheism as far back as the fifth century to
contemporary Christianity is through the bridge of the One who
said, "I am the Way." I only suggest at this point that Walker's
position cannot be taken seriously without the acknowledgment
that he is a black scholar going against the dominant traditional
European white theology. Additionally, it raises this academic
scholarly question: Is it even remotely possible that the white
missionaries were wrong? Is it possible that they brought their
European theology and refused to be confused by the facts? Is

---

62   Ibid (p. 12-13).

it possible they learned something so different they chose not to report it? (I'm just asking!)

I was only able to pass my defense of my dissertation and be awarded my doctorate by means of a compromise whereby I agreed to insert a footnote and cite in the text that Walker's position deserves further investigation. My proctor sternly looked me in the eye and admonished me, "If you leave that paragraph in there, you will *never* get a degree from this school." I knew that if I wanted to graduate, I could not win the war of not including it without the comment.

By the way, the humbling twist was that I was traveling on a speaking tour, and I would have had to turn in my document past the due date. But I was given an anonymous note instructing me to leave my last draft in the school office. The final version of my dissertation was typed by someone and returned to the office. To this day I don't know who volunteered to do that, but God is so good!

You see, I had set a goal for my life that was inspired by Dr. Martin Luther King, Jr. He was the first black man I heard of who was always called "Dr. King." I said, "One day, I'll be called that!" I wasn't about to let a footnote stop me!

My spiritual and academic journey has taught me to ground my life on the revelation of the Word of God, but I have also learned that God's Word has come down through the filters of men (primarily) with feet of clay, cultural biases, and experiential baggage. I have learned that commentators are not infallible and are not inspired on the level of biblical inspiration. As a professor once told me, "Remember, a commentary is just somebody's comment." It's not news, it's not necessarily fact, it's just a thought or an opinion.

After realizing and acknowledging the reality of the flawed humanity of theologues, gifted writers, and spiritual mentors who have helped shape my walk with the Lord and my Kingdom values over the years, one of the questions that has plagued me has been where the race and color issue come from. I affirm the excellent education I have received at institutions that were predominantly white. I know what it's like to be the only face of color in a classroom or on a dorm floor.

My own personal experiences with racism and bias are always overshadowed by my gratitude to the Lord, who always overrules any fleeting thoughts of wishing I had traveled a different road. I know, and have been told and taught, that one's ethnicity and race is secondary to being a Kingdom dweller. The most significant dialogues I have engaged in (which are almost always in a group of my right-leaning comrades) have always evolved—or devolved—into the position that color and race don't matter. I have a friend who proudly declares, "I am Christian first and black second." That sounds really spiritual, but anyone who comes into contact with him for the first time will know just by looking at him that he's black before they know he's saved.

Regarding the specific biblical commentary on racism as we know it, Dr. Cain Hope Felder makes a significant observation and contribution to the discussion:

> "Ancient authors of biblical texts did have a color consciousness (awareness of certain physiological differences), but this consciousness of color/race... was by no means a political or ideological basis for enslaving, oppressing, or in any way demeaning other peoples. In fact, the Bible contains no narratives in which the original intent was to negate the full humanity of black people or view blacks in an unfavorable way. Such negative attitudes about black people are entirely postbiblical."[63]

---

63   Felder, Cain Hope, editor. *Stoney The Road We Trod: African American Biblical Interpretations.* Minneapolis: Fortress Press 1991. Pg 127.

I have been taught that the Bible is about a loving God, the history of His people, and the salvation offered through His Son. It is not a history of mankind. It is not a history book.

I remember the first time I was in a class where the name of Flavius Josephus was referenced. I learned that this first-century Jewish historian is often cited as an "extra-biblical" source to give most often validation of various biblical revelations. Josephus was a "1st Century Jewish politician, soldier, and historian, whose writings constitute important sources for our understanding of biblical history and of the political history of Roman Palestine in the 1st Century C.E."[64] The *Tyndale Bible Dictionary* says Josephus was witness to many of the events about which he wrote. His works illumine the period in which the church came into existence, especially concerning the religion, politics, geography, and prominent persons of the early Christian era. Of particular interest to Christians are his references to John the Baptist, Jesus, and James the Just (Jesus' brother).[65]

Josephus is significant for the Bible reader because his four surviving works, in 30 volumes, provide our main avenue for information about the environment in which Christianity was born. He is the only contemporary author outside the New Testament to write in any detail about the Jerusalem temple and priesthood, the Roman governors (including Pontius Pilate), the countryside of Judea and Galilee, the various groups and factions in Jewish society, and even such figures as John the Baptist and Jesus' brother James. (Josephus also has a passage on Jesus, but the version that survives is inauthentic.) His extensive biblical paraphrase (*Ant. 1-11*) is an extremely valuable example of Jewish biblical interpretation at the time of the New Testament.

---

64 Feldman, L. H. Josephus (Person), D.N. Freedman (Ed.), *The Anchor Yale Bible Dictionary*; Doubleday, New York (1992; Vol. 3, p. 981).
65 Elwell, W. A., and Comfort, P. W. *Tyndale Bible Dictionary*; Tyndale House Publishers, Wheaton, IL (2001, p. 738).

We seldom hear information about the gap between the Old Testament and the new. Flavius Josephus helps fill is some of the blanks of the latter time just before the biblical account picks up the story with the Gospels. It is significant that he was not personally connected to the apostles or gospel writings, which validates his contributions even more as secular support for the divine story. I will say more about Josephus when we look again at the so-called curse of Ham.

I am a fanatical proponent of understanding the culture and context of the biblical story. I have lost count of the number of times I have been to Israel. Two trips changed my life. My first trip to South Africa was a connection with my ethnic roots. My first trip to Israel will always be the one where I found a connection with my spiritual roots. I love that country. However, my inquisitive mind asks questions about biblical issues that are not found in the Bible. This obviously doesn't elevate cultural history or traditions and customs above the spiritual value of biblical revelation. But I am intrigued with discovering background information that gives me valuable insight into the biblical story. The InterVarsity Press *New Bible Dictionary* says this about Josephus:

> "The works of Josephus provide indispensable background material for the student of late intertestamental and NT history. In them we meet many figures, both Jewish and Gentile, who are well known to us from the NT. Sometimes his writings supply a direct commentary on NT references, *e.g.* on the mention of Judas of Galilee in Acts 5:37 and of the *'Egyptian' in Acts 21:38. It is unlikely, however, that his works were known to any NT writer. Of special interest are his references to John the Baptist (*Ant. 18.116ff*), to James the Lord's brother (*Ant. 20.200*), and to our Lord (*Ant. 18.63f.*)—a passage which, while it has been subjected to some Christian editing, is basically authentic."[66]

66   Bruce, F.F., Josephus, Flavius. D.R.W. Wood, I.H. Marshall, A.R. Millard, J.I. Packer, and D.J. Wiseman (Eds.), *New Bible Dictionary*. InterVarsity Press, Leicester, England; Downers

It has been suggested that some of Josephus' writings that validated Christ as Messiah were "edited" by Christian historians in order to build a historical case for the divinity of Jesus. I have learned that the true seeker of truth is not encumbered by the source of that truth. Josephus is a source of historical and first century cultural influence who adds significant non-biblical supplemental support for divine revelation. Here are three important conclusions about Josephus and Jesus from the online blog website JonathanMorrow.org:

1. Josephus was a 1st century Jewish historian who talked about Jesus (and his brother James cf. Antiquities 20.200).
2. This passage (Antiquities 18:63-64) is disputed and likely does contain some Christian interpolations (fancy word for some Christian edits or embellishments). You need to be aware of this, so you are not blindsided by this skeptical challenge to Jesus. Knowing this finer point of history will also give you more credibility in the conversation.
3. Recognizing some Christian edits does not remove the historical core of what Josephus believed about Jesus. We are still on solid footing citing Josephus as a significant source of extra-biblical evidence for the historical Jesus. In fact, this text in Josephus removes any doubt that Jesus actually existed.[67]

There is clearly some dispute about the validity of Josephus as a Christian. The Morrow site also states, "The early Church father Origen believed that Josephus was never converted."[68] However, again,

Grove, IL (1996; 3rd ed., p. 611).
67  Blog story titled "What Did the Jewish Historian Josephus Really Say About Jesus? 3 Things Every Christian Should Know About Josephus and Jesus." See: https://www. jonathanmorrow.org/what-did-the-jewish-historian-josephus-really-say-about-jesus/
68  Ibid.

that adds credibility for me. Josephus is a historian who validates Jesus with no special spiritual agenda. It is clear that Josephus is a non-biblical source of Jesus as a historical figure with influence and impact on the times in which he lives. Again, the Morrow site states:

> "At this time there was a wise man who was called Jesus. And his conduct was good, and [he] was known to be virtuous. And many people from among the Jews and the other nations became his disciples. Pilate condemned Him to be crucified and to die. And those who had become his disciples did not abandon his discipleship. They reported that he had appeared to them three days after his crucifixion and that he was alive. Accordingly, he was perhaps the Messiah concerning whom the prophets have recounted wonders. (10th Century Arabic Text.)"[69]

It was the realization of the value of extra-biblical sources that prompted me to include secular resources for my search for understanding, with the hope of gaining a broader picture of the greatness of God and the miracle of the Word of God, particularly in relation to the issue of race and ethnic relations. This may seem like an excursion into irrelevant waters, but my purpose is to highlight the value I place on Scripture and supportive resources that affirm biblical truth. We must always stand on the value and power of the Word of God first and foremost, keeping in mind that resources like Josephus don't carry the same weight as the Word of God. We must never disqualify a truth because of its non-inclusion in the canon.

On the other hand, we must also acknowledge the salvific goal of Scripture. In Romans 1:16 Paul said that the Word of God contains the gospel, which is the very power of God unto salvation, and not just for the Jew but to the Gentile also. I understand that intellectually

---

69    Ibid.

and spiritually I am a Gentile (as a non-Jew), but there have been seasons in my life when I have wondered if that "power of God unto salvation" really includes me. Even though I accept the gospel Paul speaks of, the world in which I live has often implied (sometimes subtly, sometimes overtly) that I am in another category. Or, at best, I'm a second-class citizen of the Kingdom of God. Add to that the cultural confirmation that I am on the fringes, in the margins, and even outside the circle of His glory, and my confusion can be compounded.

There is a famous picture of a black spiritual giant named William J. Seymour, sitting in the hall of a Bible class taught by a white prophet and leader in what became known as Pentecostalism. I fully understand this related passage in Robert Longman's *Azusa Street Timeline*:

> "In 1905, one of Parham's students, Lucy Farrow, paved the way for Parham to teach some courses in Houston, Texas. One of those she sent to him was one William Seymour, a black who was apparently about to become a minister in the Church of God (Anderson, IN). According to the segregation law and the landlord, and enforced by Parham, Seymour had to sit in the hallway instead of the classroom because he was African American."[70]

At 71 years old, I look at life differently. When you realize you have lived longer than you thought you would live, your attitude and viewpoint shift. I journey down the highway of life with two pieces of glass in front of me: a little rearview mirror and a broad windshield. The windshield shows me where I'm going, and the rearview mirror shows me where I've been. The windshield is bigger than the rearview mirror. As I look back, I see flashbacks of seasons when I have felt

70   Longman, Robert; *Azusa Street Timeline: The Apostolic Faith Mission, Pentecostalist History*. (1997-2013; www.Spirithome.com).

like W. J. Seymour sitting in the hallway, trying to soak up all the knowledge he could. In my life, I have felt like I was often invited in but not all the way in. I have bowed to the powers that be. I have played the game to be accepted. I have even compromised who I really am in order to appear that I am who I'm not.

I heard a little rhyme when I was a teenager that succinctly expresses this internal, incessant confusion and turmoil of identity:

> *"Be who you is;*
> *not who you ain't.*
> *Cause if you is who you ain't*
> *you ain't who you is!"*

I have been through seasons where I wasn't sure who I really was because I was trying so hard to be someone I wasn't. I don't think I was playing masquerade. I think I was trying to be more of who I thought people needed me to be in order to accept me into their lives and their circles. Only I find out there was a limit to how far they would let me in.

Don't read this as a complaint or a sad tale. It's more of a story of victory. A story of triumph or of liberty. It's about accepting myself with the knowledge that the Lord God of the World loves me just the way I am. He did not make a mistake when He made me. He did not use the wrong color. He did not put me in the wrong family. I am *intentional*. I am on purpose. I am loved by the God of my salvation. I am loved just the way I am.

And He lovingly made you and knew you even before you were in your mother's womb. He—the Great I Am, Who lovingly clothed you with the temporary flesh you wear—loves you too. To this very day and always. Just the way your are.

Oh, that the whole world would get that profound and simple truth! God makes no mistakes.

# 5

# THE CHURCH DOORS ARE OPEN

*We half-stumbled along, holding onto each other in the crowd, which was mostly silent now but for the whimpers, sobs, and occasional defiant shouts of "BLACK POWER!"—the anthem that had sprung from the philosophical differences between Malcolm X and Dr. King, and was paraphrased by James Brown's anthem, "Say it Loud. I'm Black, and I'm Proud." Scenes like these would soon birth the angry chant, "No justice, no peace!" which would become the mantra of the justice fighters of the generation.*

*But the abrupt, painful cries of those in our group occasionally shouting "Black Power!" were most frightening because their shouts were quickly followed by the sickening thud of billy club on bone and then...silence.*

*My girlfriend and I stayed quiet and kept shuffling...*

\* \* \*

Peter fairly exploded with his good news in Acts 10:34-35. "It's God's own truth, nothing could be plainer: God plays no favorites! It makes no difference who you are or where you're from—if you want God and are ready to do as He says, the door is open."[71] (*The Message*)

There is a tradition in the African American Baptist church that is exercised every Sunday. It comes at the end of the sermon. First of all, almost every message ends with Jesus going to the cross and rising on Sunday morning. In fact, I have heard some of the old

---

71    Peterson, Eugene H.; *The Message: The Bible in Contemporary Language* (2002).

preachers in the African American tradition say, "If you don't take Jesus to the grave and get Him up, you haven't preached!" So, you knew the message was coming to the end when the preacher would say something like, "They marched Him to a hill called Calvary. They put Him on an old rugged cross. They put nails in His hands and rivets in His feet. They hung Him high, stretched Him wide and He dropped His head in the locks of His shoulders. And He died! Didn't He die! They took Him down and put Him in a borrowed tomb. He stayed all night Friday night. He stayed there all day Saturday. He stayed there all night Saturday night. But EARLY! EARLY (You have to say it twice.) Sunday morning, He got up with all power in heaven and earth in His hands!"

And when the celebration and joy of the resurrection began to subside, the preacher would say, "The door of the church is open!" This was what some called "the invitation" or "the call to discipleship." It was a cultural ethnic paraphrase of Jesus saying, "Follow me." It was the opportunity for those who were not saved, who had not accepted Jesus Christ as Lord and Savior, to do so. "THE DOOR IS OPEN," would sometimes be followed by "Whosoever will, let Him come." But everyone knew anything and everything that had been said prior to this was but preparation for this event, the highlight of the service, the opening of the doors of the church to receive anyone and everyone who would say, "Yes," to the Lord.

An old song in the African American spiritual genre by an unknown composer that speaks of the greatness of the love of God goes like this:

> *My God is so high*
> *So high -*
> *You can't get over Him;*
> *So wide -*
> *You can't get around Him;*

*So low -*
*You can't get under Him,*
*You mus' go through the door.*

The implied "door" is Jesus who said, "I am the door."

I have since noticed the transitions and variations on this invitation tradition in other churches. There are varying degrees of formality and interpretations of this pattern of offering people the opportunity to accept Jesus Christ. In some cases, it appears to be an accepted and understood part of church culture that, although there is no formal invitation from the pulpit, the worshipers know what to do. The "what to do" also varies. In some churches, people are invited to go to a room set aside for spiritual counseling, prayer, and instruction for next steps. In some cases, there are people standing at the altar, sometimes clergy, sometimes laypeople, sometimes deacons. These servants are there to receive those who publicly come to the altar, indicating their desire to "come through the door that is open." In some cases, there are cards or forms in the pews that can be filled out in a more private response to the open door. It's a familiar procedure repeated in countless churches each Sunday, week after week, year after year.

As I have pondered this issue of racism, I have often wondered: *Is the door of the church REALLY open?* If so, how far open is it? Is it open or just cracked? Are there doorkeepers at the door to screen those who want to come in through the door?

Many years ago, I was a musician, playing at a church service in Los Angeles. I think it was a New Year's Eve service. It was back in the day when women were wearing Hot Pants (later known as Daisy Dukes), which were basically *very* short "short-shorts"—often not much wider than a belt, and were popularized and musicalized by the late great James Brown's song of the same name.

At this particular service, I recall a woman strolling in the back door wearing red hot pants in this rather large church. As she was making her way to the pew, a couple of male ushers dashed over to her and began ushering her back to the door. "I won't cause no trouble!" she pleaded as they began to struggle with her. I could hear her from my seat at the organ all the way in the front of the church, saying, "I just want to hear about Jesus—*please!*" She was obviously inebriated, but she didn't come in to make any trouble. As they guided her out, the ushers were telling her, "You can't come in here with those pants on." And she kept crying out that all she wanted was to hear about Jesus.

Is the door of the church *really* open? Is it open to the drunk lady wearing the short-shorts who wants to hear the Word? Is it open to the man or the woman dealing with homosexuality? Is it open to the immigrant struggling to find work? Is it open to those whose skin isn't the same color as yours? Is the door of the church open, *really*?

A few years ago, my wife and I took our son Kendan on a vacation to Walt Disney World in Florida. As is my habit when I'm out of town and have a Sunday off, I almost always look for a place to worship. On this particular vacation there was a large, white Baptist church, pastored by a well-known Southern Baptist minister who was also an author. I had seen him on television and run across him at conferences. So, I went in and sat in the ground floor area about eight or nine rows from the back of the middle section, on the end. The church, which had a beautiful wraparound balcony, was the largest church building I had ever been in.

As the service progressed, everyone was encouraged to greet their neighbor, as is customary in many churches. The first thing I noticed was that no one, *not one single person*, even turned in my direction. No one in front, no one behind, no one across the aisle from me. It was if I were the invisible man—right there in the middle of their own church. I could tell that many of the parishioners knew one another, which meant that a lot of them could probably figure out I was a visitor. But their obvious neglect to acknowledge my presence caught me so much off-guard that I couldn't bring myself to push the issue by inserting myself into their personal "space" while they were so busy ignoring me. As I looked around at all these smiling people, hugging one another and shaking hands, I felt a little like a party crasher. But it was the second thing I noticed that may have contained a clue to their behavior: as far as I could see, I was the only black person in the entire assembly. When someone finally spoke to me, it was a kind, young, hippy-looking dude who invited me to a fellowship after the service.

So, I wonder: Is the door of the church really open?

There is a passage in Acts 10 that has a personal application for me. Careful exegesis of this verse echoes my personal journey. In his book *Acts of The Apostles*, D.G. Peterson writes:

> "Peter begins the fourth of his messages in Acts (cf. 2:14–39; 3:12–26; 4:8–12) with another remarkable confession: *'I now realize how true it is (ep' alētheia katalambanomai,* 'truly I am coming to realize') *that God does not show favoritism (ouk estin prosōpolēmptēs ho theos,* 'God is not one to show partiality')'*. The vision given to Peter (vv. 10–16), together with the realisation that God had been communicating directly with Cornelius (vv. 30–33), has led him to this conclusion. Peter now sees this biblical teaching 'more sharply and more clearly, for it is being demonstrated in a new way'. A key text on this theme is Deuteronomy 10:17–19. Although God gave a special status and role to Israel (e.g. Ex. 19:5–6), he declared His intention to bless the nations through His chosen people (e.g. Gn. 12:3)."[72]

72  Peterson, D. G. *The Acts of the Apostles.* William B. Eerdmans Publishing Company Grand Rapids, MI; Nottingham, England (2009; pp. 334–335).

*The Message* Bible version of Acts 10:34 says, "Peter fairly exploded." In other words, he was excited because he just got it. It was one of those *Aha!* moments. Same as when Paul got it, and he too fairly exploded with his "good news" of the gospel. Peter too explodes with excitement that in "God's own truth, nothing could be plainer; it's God's truth that God plays no favorites." One of the handicaps of reading and interpreting Scripture is that the texts don't always communicate the emotions and feelings behind a given text. *The Message* version tries to capture the excitement of Paul. "I get it!" Peter proclaims, "God does not show favorites! I get it now!"

I am almost ashamed to admit that I used to think God was prejudiced. I used to think the dynamics of racism in the world, and especially in my little world growing up in E. St. Louis, were according to the will of God. I used to think, "That's just the way God made it." Deal with it. I thought it was part of my challenge to accept this as the will of God. I used to think it was a demonstration of my faith to just trust God that the schisms in His creation were all part of His will. It's just the way it is. Trust Him on the issue; He knows why He's doing it.

I also remember when I changed that idea about God and realized He is not prejudiced, and it happened through a relationship and precious friendship. A man I am honored to call a friend is Pastor Frederick K. C. Price, founder of Crenshaw Christian Center. Long before I had the honor of meeting him, Dr. Price led the people of his congregation to build The Faith Dome. It was built at a cost of around $15,000,000 and seated over 10,000. I had never heard of anyone with such great faith and a big vision— definitely not a black man, with that kind of faith in God, who I previously thought was prejudiced. Oh, I had seen huge churches for white congregations. By then I had heard of or even visited a few churches that looked more like arenas than houses of worship. But none were led by a black man. It was through Dr. Price that I learned God is not prejudiced.

In my humbled spirit I declared the words of Peter in Acts 10:34: "I now realize how true it is that God does not show favoritism." (NIV) The example displayed in this passage in the 10th chapter of Acts reveals a principle that is quite possibly one of the most (if not the *single most*) significant illustration in all of Scripture related to the revelation of the will of God (who is a God of reconciliation) with regard to the issue of race and ethnic division and the challenge of racial reconciliation in these last and evil days of the United States of America.

And it began with two visions by two men who had never met one another. They were about to. In a most unusual way.

Peter's vision occurred around noon when he was praying on the roof of a house where he was staying in Joppa. He was tired and hungry from his travels, and he fell asleep and dreamed about food.

Have you ever been so tired and so hungry that you dreamed about food? In his sleep, Peter dreamed about food, and in a vision, God showed him a sheet. Some folk call it a blanket, but he rolled down this sheet and on this sheet were all kinds of animals meant to be eaten. The Bible says there were "all kinds of four-footed animals, as well as reptiles of the earth and birds of the air." (Acts 10:12-13; NIV) When I look at that menu a little closer, I have to admit, there's some stuff on there that I probably wouldn't eat either. But he looked over the animals on the sheet and the voice of God said, "Rise, Peter. Slay and eat." Here's God's showing him the sheet with all these different animals, but the problem is that in this group of animals, there are animals that a good Jew would not eat. And so, God told him to rise and eat because he was hungry. *I've got something for you. Pick anything on the menu, and eat it.*

The conversation might have gone something like this:

"Well, now, look, Lord, I've never eaten or touched some of these things on this sheet in my whole life. I cannot eat some of this stuff. As a matter of fact, Lord, you told me *not* to eat some of this stuff. I'm a Jew. I only eat kosher. I'll pass. I'm good."

And God replies, "Well, if I say it's okay to eat, it's okay to eat." This exchange went on for three rounds. In fact, it never says Peter agreed to eat. Maybe he ate when the vision ended or he woke up. It's as if the Lord was saying, *Okay, Peter. You are a slow learner. You don't get it. So, if this vision doesn't work for you, let's try real life.* *The Message* Bible continues the story in Acts 10:15-18:

> "The voice came a second time: 'If God says it's okay, it's okay.' This happened three times, and then the blanket was pulled back up into the skies. As Peter, puzzled, sat there trying to figure out what it all meant, the men sent by Cornelius showed up at Simon's front door."[73]

Two days earlier, completely unknown to Peter, Cornelius, a centurion and officer in charge of 100 men in the Italian Regiment stationed in Caesarea under the command of the Roman Empire, had a vision. In his vision, God said to Cornelius, "Your prayers and gifts to the poor have come up as a memorial offering before God. Now go and send for a man named Simon, who is called Peter. He's staying in the house of Simon the Tanner, down the road in a seaside village called Joppa."

So, this first vision, seen by the centurion Cornelius in Caesarea, set the stage for the second vision, seen by Peter, who happened to be in Joppa, down the road from Caesarea, which is about 75 miles north of Jerusalem. Keep in mind this is the same Peter from Acts chapter 2, the same Peter who preached on the Day of Pentecost, the same Peter under the power of the Holy Spirit on the Day of Pentecost, and who is now here in chapter 10 of Acts. He has been traveling around, dealing with believers in the first church, and he came to Joppa, where he was staying with Simon the Tanner.

---

73  Peterson, Eugene H.; *The Message: The Bible in Contemporary Language* (2002).

Now we fast forward to the scene in the house of Cornelius, phase two of the revelation about the God who shows no favorites, after Cornelius sends for Peter. Now it makes more sense to hear Peter *finally* say, "Oh. Now I get it, God. Now I realize You are no respecter of persons. You don't play favorites; you're not prejudiced." Peter acknowledges the God who doesn't play favorites through the move of the Holy Spirit in the life of Cornelius and agrees to go visit Cornelius to hear what he wants to tell Peter. I love the way Peterson paraphrases it in *The Message*: Peter said, "God has just shown me that no race is better than any other."

So, the day after Peter's vision, he found himself at the house of Cornelius, the centurion he had never met. Acts 10:27 begins at Cornelius's front door, where the centurion greeted the apostle, and the two men talk things over as they enter the house: "Talking with him [Cornelius], Peter went inside and found a large gathering of people" (NIV). Peter, a Jew, was now going into a house full of non-Jews, a house of Gentiles. When they entered this house, Cornelius introduced Peter to everyone gathered there. I love what Peter says: "You know, this is highly irregular." Jews don't visit, relax, hang out and kick it with people of another race. *We Jews don't roll like that. We don't fellowship and socialize with folk like you.* Indeed, the *New International Version* puts it even more tersely: "You are well aware that it is against our law for a Jew to associate with a Gentile or visit him." In other words, *Just being here with you could cause me some trouble.*

Yet, after announcing that the get-together was highly irregular and against Jewish law, Peter added, "But God has shown me that I should not call any man impure or unclean." (NIV) In other words, God had shown him in a vision just a day earlier that no race was better than any other. "So, when I was sent for," he continued, "I came without raising any objection. May I ask why you sent for me?" And as Cornelius lead him into the room filled with Gentiles, he explained the vision he had the previous day—a vision that caused the powerful centurion Cornelius to send for the powerful apostle Peter, men who had never met. And Peter not only told those gathered all about Jesus of Nazareth and all He did, but the Holy Spirit came upon all of those in the room. God's plan in the unusual meeting was simple: theology meets sociology meets ministry equals walls coming down and doors opening up.

Here's the valuable principle we must learn: our theology informs our anthropology, and our anthropology informs our sociology. That is, your theology—what you believe about God, how you regard God, what you know about Him, how you see and value Him and the position He has in your life—will impact, inform, and speak into your anthropology, your concept of *people*, how you deal with other individuals, how you sociologically and socially interact in relationship with others, as well as how you "do" community, how you comport yourself in life, what kind of neighborhood you build and contribute to, what sort of family you make.

Then, adding another link in the chain, God says in Second Corinthians that you and I are ministers of reconciliation. In other words, we have been reconciled and are therefore called to the ministry of reconciliation. So, here's how it flows:

- Your theology impacts your anthropology (how you view people).
- Your anthropology impacts your sociology (how you interact with people).
- Your sociology impacts your view on the ministry of reconciliation (how you value bringing about and seeing people walking in unity).

So, what exactly is reconciliation? Let me give you three broad strokes. First of all, reconciliation has to do with *the removal of walls* or those things that separate us. Reconciliation paints a picture of a wall, separating a group on one side from a group on the other side. The removal of that wall of separation brings the people on both sides together. It produces unity among the people. It is a coming together after the walls of separation have been removed. It results in reconciliation.

Second, reconciliation is *the restoration of favor.* It is when justice has been satisfied. When honor has been restored. When favor has been renewed and bestowed upon all, despite which side of the fence they were on. This restoration of the favor of relationship, of valuing those on either side of the fence is the elimination of whatever was causing the wall of separation between them.

The third thing is that reconciliation is *a repositioning or changing of a previous position.* That is, people who at one time were separated or kept at a distance from one another because of the walls or issue that formerly separated them, are reunited when those walls are removed. They are now repositioned into a place that brings them value and high regard. Thus, reconciliation is all about removing, restoring, and repositioning.

A brilliant African-American theologian by the name of Dr. Brenda McNeil, a professor at Seattle Pacific University, wrote a book I highly recommend. It's titled *Roadmap to Reconciliation.* In this must-read book, Dr. McNeil quotes Emmanuel Katongole and Chris Rice that "reconciliation is God's language for a broken world" and defines reconciliation as "an ongoing spiritual process involving forgiveness, repentance and justice that restores broken relationships and systems to reflect God's original intention for all creation to flourish."[74]

However, I suggest that racial reconciliation has a problem. Etymologically, the root understanding of the word "reconciliation" comes with an assumption that at one time there was conciliation

---

74  McNeil, Brenda Salter. *Roadmap to Reconciliation: Moving Communities into Unity, Wholeness and Justice.* InterVarsity Press. Kindle Edition. Location 198 of 1902.

which has now become a restoration of a previous unity. Being reconciled assumes that at one time there was a division, a split, a disagreement, that separated and divided.

Paul's classic passage on reconciliation is found in Second Corinthians 5:18, where the context is spiritual reconciliation to God. The word Paul uses speaks of being "restored to the favor of God, to recover God's favor."[75] This favor would be pictured when our creation parents, Adam and Eve, were in the favor of God; back when God looked at them and said, "It is very good." The obvious favor and blessing that is pronounced and contained in the "very good" of God also includes a truth that could be easily overlooked. The tendency is usually to focus on the "very good" reserved for the creation of Man, with a forward look to how this relationship is both honored by the stewardship of the garden and then broken by disobedience. However, there is a more encompassing revelation, one that comes from Rabbi Samson Raphael Hirsch, who notes this with divine insight:

> "...Every single creation is good, but only now, when the series of creations is closed, and each single one can be considered in relation to the whole, everything is not only good, but very good. (Good) is not only the conception of plurality "all," that therein everyone is included and none left out, but (good) is a conception of the union of the plurality, is many looked on as a single unit, not so much "all" as "the whole."[76]

Rabbi Hirsch notes that the word for "good" is related to a primitive root from which comes the concept of *completion*, of wholeness in the sense of a completed circle; something that is round, a ring, a hoop, a wreath, a crown.

---

75  *Thayer's Greek Lexicon*, PC Study Bible formatted Electronic Database. Biblesoft, Inc. (2006).

76  Hirsch, Samson Raphael. *The Pentateuch, Vol 1. Genesis.* Gateshead: Judaica Press. Ltd. 1989. P38.

"The circle is naught but the most complete line, that space that is ruled with the same measure of force from one point in every conceivable direction. A circle is therefore a pregnant expression for the whole sphere that a being can control from his own standpoint. Hence all the expressions for the conception of completion and perfection are related in Hebrew to the word 'circle.'"[77]

The revelation is that the "very good" of man is most significant in that it is the culmination of God's intent for unity in creation. The theology of reconciliation in Paul is the spiritual return to the creative concept of unity "in the beginning." It is restoration of the plan of God for unity and oneness in His creation.

Reconciliation, then, contains and implies the assumption that you go back to a point where there was once unity. For example, Paul argues that spiritually we were one with God, and that oneness was destroyed and was damaged because of sin. The goal of reconciliation is to remove the issue of sin that has divided us, so we can then be back in unity and oneness with God. How do we do that? Paul says we can be reconciled with God because the issue that divided us—which was sin—was dealt with when Jesus hung on a cross between two thieves and died, granting forgiveness of our sin, therefore removing it, and we are now one with Him.

But if that's the principle, then I suggest that *racial reconciliation* is an oxymoron, because it comes with a false assumption, that of returning to some point where there was once racial oneness. This is an oxymoron, because in the United States of America there has *never* been racial harmony in this land of the free and home of the brave. There's no previous position of racial equality, justice and harmony to be reconciled back to, because the status quo that masqueraded as unity was this: *I know my place; you know your place. You stay in your place; I'll stay in my place.*

---

77   Ibid.

*And let's call it, "Let's all get along."* It has always been a tenuous tolerance forever on the verge of erupting when one side or the other overstepped the bounds of that false unity, which was erected by a pact engineered by the devil.

The painful truth is that the history of our country has been constructed upon a hierarchy that places some on the top and some on the bottom, where those on the bottom struggle for equity to see those above, let alone pass or be on the top. So, if the idea of reconciliation means to go back to a previous assumption, it's a false assumption in the natural. At best the assumed unity has been vertical in which whiteness was always on the top of the social and economic hierarchy. Yet, fortunately for us all, there is a God and there is the power of the Spirit of the living God that can cross every barrier, bring down every wall, cross every division, bring unity where there has been division, make a way out of no way, and open the door where there is no door by the power of the living God.

The issue of racial reconciliation has to do with how we relate to one another after the walls have come down. But racial reconciliation will never happen until people initiate and release the power of God to move in their lives, through their lives, and touch somebody else's life and bring unity, at least in that circle in which God has placed them.

The walls come down when the clarion call of the contemporary prophetess Diana Ross goes into action, who called on us to "Reach out and touch somebody's hand, and make this world a better place, if you can." When we metaphorically and actually reach out and touch somebody's hand, that's when the possibility rears up for us to be involved in making this world a better place. It matters not what color that hand is. Matters not what ethnicity that hand is. Matters not what persuasion that hand represents. Reconciliation starts with a *touch*. A touch of the love of the living God. A touch of invitation into the family of the God of the creation of unity and oneness.

Reconciliation is always on the other side of *forgiveness*. The frustrating truth is that one can forgive and not be reconciled. Possibly that principle is no more painfully illustrated than it often is in the relationship of a man and a woman who are married, when the marriage gets in trouble, and there's an issue that has caused an offense that at some point will need forgiveness. If humility doesn't take hold and that forgiveness doesn't take place, that marriage, that relationship, is doomed.

However, even if forgiveness is granted, that forgiveness may or may not lead to reconciliation. This is because the issue of reconciliation has to do with *going back to the point of unity in that relationship*, and the painful reality is that often there is forgiveness, yet that relationship has been so damaged that reconciliation cannot be renewed. In domestic cases like that, often the most attainable priority may then be, "I forgive you. You forgive me. How do we take care of our children," rather than, "Let's go back and do a renewal of our vows."

We probably all know of examples of positive, productive co-parenting by ex-spouses, where they lay aside the challenges that split them up, and they take care of that baby, those children, that family. But the forgiveness does not always lead to the reconciliation if reconciliation means *let's go back down that aisle*. You have to go farther than a stroll down an aisle in an effort to reconnect with a former selfless togetherness. Time may heal, but time can also accumulate hurts that must be dealt with at some point before reconciliation may commence. Forgiveness may lead to peace, but peace does not always lead to reconciliation.

With God, true reconciliation means, *I forgive you; you've been forgiven, and I will love you the way I did before you did what hurt my heart and what caused me to have to forgive you in the first place.* You can break God's heart, but you can't break God's love.

Sin breaks God's heart, but sin cannot break God's love for the sinner. So, God says, "I will remember your sins no more." That's spiritual reconciliation. God does not say, "I will forget them." He says, "I will remember your sins no more." But how can an omnipotent, omniscient God forget? It raises a theological question. The revelation of truth is that the all-powerful God has the power to limit His own memory. An omnipotent God can inflict Himself with temporary amnesia:

> "There are three groups of meanings: 1) for completely inward mental acts such as 'remembering' or 'paying attention to,' 2) for such inward mental acts accompanied by appropriate external acts, and 3) for forms of audible speaking with such meanings as 'recite' or 'invoke.' Cognate evidence indicates that the third group of meanings is closest to the verb's root meaning. This range of meanings shows the same blending or overlapping between mental states and external acts seen also in other Hebrew terms (e.g. Hebrew...'to hear')."[78]

He does have the power to remember what He wants to remember because "remember" does not mean to erase and to forget as we define it. God says He will remember no more. He will no longer deliberately recall it to memory, dwell on it, think about it. "Remember no more" means that when He sees it, He won't hold it against you. He has dismissed it and has forgiven you and is going to treat you as though you never did it. Not because you didn't do it but because you know you did it and God knows you did it. But God says, "I am going to love you, and I'm going to bless you, and I'm going to favor you as though you never did it. Because when I forgive you, I will remember your sins no more." That's what unconditional *love* is all about—it doesn't hold you hostage to a perpetual recitation of the infraction.

So, when reconciliation comes down, God says, "I will remove that barrier, and I have forgiven you." And we will become one again with Him, because of the grace of God, the love of Christ, and the blood of Calvary.

But how does that work in the earth realm? Go back to the book of Acts, chapter 10, where Peter saw a vision of the animals lowering down in the big sheet, and he argued with God, saying, "I can't eat that because of my tradition, God. My culture says that's unclean, and I can't even touch it because my tradition and my culture says it's off limits," but then, from that repartee between him and God, Peter is able to understand the vision as God saying, "God is no respecter of persons." One version says, "God does not play favorites." Look at verse 34 very carefully because there's a revelation and a blessing in the tense of the verb. In verse 34, one version has Peter saying, "I perceive." One says, "I realize." And another one says, "I now realize." Verse 34 says, "I now realize," which is in the present active tense, which means this: *I am now realizing.* Put another way, Peter is saying, "Oh, I see it. Now I get it." Stated more in the vernacular, "Oh, that's the way you roll, God. You have no respect of persons—and I see that, because you just sent me, a Jewish man, all that stuff to eat that my tradition says is unclean."

Peter has basically stopped thinking like Peter and started thinking more spiritually, more in line with what God was teaching him about Himself.

Do you ever think more *you* than Christian? Do you think more ethnic than spiritual? Are you more black than saved? Are you more white than saved? Are you more Latino than saved? More American than saved? More one political party or the other than saved? Many are.

Peter had prioritized his ethnicity, his tradition, and his culture above what the Lord tells us to do or not to do. In effect,

God says to Peter, "I didn't ask you who your mama or daddy was. I said *eat it*, Pete. I didn't ask you what your tradition was, and if I made it, it's got to be clean. No? Would I ever tell you to do something you don't have the capacity to do? Don't ever call what I made clean unclean. Don't let your ethnicity overrule your spirituality when thus says the Lord. That's *dangerous*, Pete."

And that's exactly what it seems the white church and white America has been doing for centuries: telling God they don't really care what His Word clearly says. It seems their tradition and color and culture and grandmother and Confederate flag and all that, says, "I can't let you in. You're not white!" God says, "Look man, if I made it, if I made him, if I made her, I don't care what color, creed, or ethnicity they may be. When I open up the door, everybody's coming in!" Don't ever let your ethnicity overrule your spirituality.

Here's what Peter teaches us (and it's a lesson for me personally, as well): Peter says, "I get it." Present active is this: "I'm understanding. Oh, wow, now I realize. Now, I'm getting it. That's the way God works." God always responds based on His favor and not based on our faith, because God is no respecter of persons, and does not play favorites. God has given us the ministry of reconciliation. So Peter comes into this room with all these non-Jewish people and says, effectively, "Now I realize God doesn't deal with us according to race."

He then went to share the gospel and the story of Jesus dying on Calvary to save the sins of the world—Jews and Gentiles. When he shared the gospel, one version says, "While he was yet talking," the Holy Ghost fell and everybody in the place, including the non-Jewish Gentiles were filled with the Spirit, began to speak in other tongues and began to glorify God. Then Peter says, "Oh, my goodness. Not only did God do it again, He did it the same way he did it at the prototype, at the original gathering at the Day of Pentecost, pouring out the same gifts by the same power of the same Holy Ghost. God didn't play favorites." He doesn't have first class blessings for first-class people and second-class blessings for second class people. He doesn't have *any* classes of people. Peter realized there was now unity and reconciliation in that room by the power and the manifestation of the visitation of the Holy Spirit of the living God.

My prayer is that there would be a fresh outpouring, a fresh wind, a fresh move of God that would bring together that which we cannot do in the earth realm, but that by God's power would move and manifest reconciliation to His own honor and glory.

It began with a vision. That vision released a visitation and a manifestation of the Holy Spirit that brought about unity in the earth realm. The vision of the ascending Jesus was manifested on Pentecost.

God gave me a vision. I have been told it will never happen. I have seen in the spirit realm the house the Lord has allowed me to pastor. God gave me a vision, and I have seen our church, The Family of Champions, in Inglewood, California, looking more and more like heaven. Every race, every creed, every color, every language, every ethnicity and nationality coming together, shoulder by shoulder and elbow by elbow, lifting up holy hands, giving God praise. The presence of the living God is binding us all together. Because God is bigger than a color, bigger than a race, bigger than a creed, bigger than a flag, bigger than a nationality, bigger than an ethnicity. Only by the power of the living God, and I've seen it.

I have no idea how God's going to do it. I've seen it prophetically. You don't make prophecy happen. You get in position and watch prophecy happen. God has given me a vision. In my flesh, I am hesitant to document it in this book. In my flesh, I am afraid to put it down on paper. In my flesh, I am afraid to go on record with this. But I believe the Lord is going to do it.

The vision of Peter set the stage for Paul, because Peter was an apostle to the Jews, transitioning in Acts chapter 10, setting the stage for the gospel to reach the Gentiles. In chapter 11, Paul will pick it up and take it to the ends of the world. The church that was Jewish for nine chapters now became interracial.

I got a vision I've never seen before in my 70+ years of life. I have never seen it before in 40 years of ministry. I have never seen a church that was historically black by the power of God become more and more interracial. Never until now. I believe God is going to do it in the house He has graciously allowed me to pastor.

I have friends across the nation who pastor interracial churches, and every one of them began either interracial or white and became more interracial. I've never seen a church that was historically black become significantly interracial. For some reason, it's much easier for black people to attend a white church and submit to a white pastor than it is for white people to attend a black church and submit to a black pastor. But I know there is a God, and I know the power of the Holy Ghost. And I know the power of the Holy Spirit is bigger and stronger than the traditions of weak faith in the races of Americans.

And so, what we need is the power of the Holy Spirit. I don't know how to do it. I know that what Peter put in place, Paul saw come to fruition. God is going to put it in place. The generation that I serve now may be the one that will see it come to pass. The generation I stand before every week may be the next generation that sees it more than I will.

Dr. King said, "I've been to the mountaintop, and I have looked over to the other side, and I may not get there with you, but I know we're going to get there." God can do things that are greater, bigger, and better, and only God can do this. I'm trusting God to do it.

What are you trusting God to do in your life that only He can do, so that when it's done, you will know who did it? What are you trusting God to do that no one else can do? Your faith ought to always be on the precipice of faith and trust so that you are trusting God to do things that only He can do. Then when it gets done, you won't have to scratch your head trying to figure out who did it. You'll know that only God could do it, and since it got done, God was the one who did it. Because the door of His church is *definitely* open.

# 6

# RACISM IN ESPAÑOL AND EBONICS

*"For you are all sons of God through faith in Jesus Christ.*
*For as many of you as were baptized into Christ have put on Christ.*
*There is neither Jew nor Greek, there is neither slave nor free,*
*there is neither male nor female, for you are all one in Christ Jesus."*
—Galatians 3:26-28

*As the row of my fellow black students and I shuffled toward the*
*police vans in a measured cadence that sounded like we were shackled*
*at the ankles, occasionally broken by the shout of a cop yelling, "KEEP*
*MOVING!" I noticed that the beautiful, painted masterpieces that*
*donned the wall of our Southern Mansion-designed Union were*
*ripped, cut, and shredded. Who did that? I wondered.*

*They separated me from my girl and herded us all into different*
*paddy wagons. There, I learned that what had triggered this tragic,*
*violent night was when a band of "town kids" had stormed into the*
*Union and sliced up the priceless art in defiant response to the murder*
*of Dr. Martin Luther King, Jr.*

*I wondered if we'd be forced to pay for the damage when I*
*realized we had been paying for the damage of others long before that*
*caused on this night. And we would be paying long after...*

\* \* \*

I learned this little song by an unknown lyricist in Sunday
school. It is one of those little ditties that stick in your mind, and
you find yourself humming it long after Sunday:

*Jesus loves the little children,*
*All the children of the world.*
*Red and yellow, black and white,*
*All are precious in His sight,*
*Jesus loves the little children of the world.*

I also remember questioning the message in the lyrics, because I had never seen red or yellow people. I lived in a black and white world; predominantly white, but safely couched in neighborhoods of beautiful chocolate faces. I didn't see any Asians until I got to college, and there, in middle America, central Illinois, there were very few of them. I really don't remember being around brown faces until I was in the Marine Corps. I came to Los Angeles where I met several Latinos at the recruit depot in San Diego.

I remember in one of my rare quiet moments in boot camp, pondering that little Sunday school song and wondering why the song never mentions any little "brown" children of the world. I thought, *Does that mean Jesus doesn't love the brown ones?*

I was called to be the preacher of Faithful Central Missionary Baptist Church in 1982. When I came to the church, the neighborhood was around 90% black to Hispanic, leaning very heavily toward black. Today that neighborhood is almost 99% Hispanic to black, leaning well over half toward Hispanic. One of my co-pastors in that part of town said of his all-African American congregation, "We ain't changin'. Zion is not changin'!" He was speaking in terms of the shifting demographics of the neighborhood, which was, like my immediate area, becoming more and more populated by Hispanics.

This became a personal issue for me, because several times a month we would have people joining our fellowship who came from his church. The pastor and I were fairly close; in fact, he claimed me as one of his "spiritual sons." Neither he nor I ever mentioned it. He barked *Zion ain't changin!* And Zion never did. It gradually shrank from the thousands who once flocked to his church week after week, down to what might legitimately be called a large Sunday school class. The neighborhood had changed. The church hadn't.

A few months after I took on the responsibility of being the pastor at Faithful Central church, a Hispanic pastor and a couple of his leaders dropped by to talk to me. They were from a Seventh Day Adventist church and were looking for a place to worship on Saturdays. Having noticed that our facility was virtually closed on Saturdays, he asked if his young Hispanic congregation could use our building for worship on Saturdays. I was very excited because I saw it as an opportunity to build relationships with the community around us that was changing demographically.

I met with our deacons and some of our leaders to inform them of the opportunity. I was surprised at hearing their responses. Not one of them agreed that we should let the Hispanics use our empty building on Saturdays. Most memorable was the comment that one lady made, which received affirmative nods and a couple of *Amens* from the other deacons. She said something like, "Don't let them people come into our church. They will tear it up. You know how nasty they are."

Wow. I didn't know for certain if she was referring to Seventh Day Adventists or to Hispanics, but I was pretty sure she meant the latter. I wasn't expecting that; it caught me off guard. When the Hispanic pastor came back the next week, I told him with tears in my eyes, "Sir, I'm very sorry. They won't let me do it." I won't go into how that incident shaped my leadership style, but I remember thinking, "Lord, forgive them, for they know not what they do."

That wall was never breached, and I never saw that Hispanic brother again.

There is probably no hotter topic in our country right now than the issue of immigration. There was once a time in America when we actually touted our openness to immigrants and acknowledged that we are a nation of immigrants. One of the walls that the enemy has erected is the separation and often isolation of the Hispanic community. At the time I began writing this book, the topic of immigration had created a set of buzz words that almost everyone knew was code for primarily Latinos and Hispanics seeking a new life in this land of the free and home of the brave. *Immigration. Walls. Fences. Borders.* These are almost always words used to directly or indirectly refer to the Spanish speaking or Latino heritage of men and women and boys and girls attempting to respond to the heretofore standing invitation to "Give me your tired, your poor, Your huddled masses yearning to breathe free."[79] In light of the politicization of this issue of racism that hangs over our country like a damp, moldy blanket, it raises the same issue we reviewed in the previous chapter: how open are the doors to this nation, really? Has our liberty welcome become an empty platitude? Are people truly welcome to immigrate to America? Should France repossess the Statue of Liberty or just have the motto altered or removed?

On the other hand, I believe the present state of our society does raise several urgent questions, foremost of which is *Where is the church?* What is the voice of the church in these calamitous days across our nation? Does the church have a voice in this matter? Is the church even at the table? Is reconciliation related to Hispanic Americans an issue that the church is mandated to manifest? Does the biblical commission to be ambassadors of reconciliation apply on any level to the plight of Hispanic Americans? Does the biblical anecdote of the good Samaritan apply to Christians any longer?

There is a valuable principle of priority revealed in Luke's

---

79  Hunter, Walt; January 16, 2018, story in *The Atlantic* titled "The Story Behind the Poem on the Statue of Liberty."

version of the Great Commission, where Jesus says, "You shall be witnesses to Me in Jerusalem, and in all Judea and Samaria, and to the end of the earth." (Acts 1:8 NIV) The first stage of expansion of the gospel, then, would be from Jerusalem to Judea. Jerusalem was home base. Josephus, the first century Jewish historian, gives geographical descriptions of the district, the territory of Judea.[80] It is significant to note that the instructions of the Lord were to begin in Jerusalem. Jerusalem was home. There was work to be done in their own neighborhoods, in their own city. That rings true for me as a resident in Los Angeles.

If you live in L.A., you don't have to go anywhere to do "missions work." You can just go across town, or in many cases around the corner or across the street. From the website World Population Review:

"Los Angeles is an incredibly diverse city, home to people from over 140 countries who speak 224 languages that have been identified. Ethnic communities like Koreatown, Chinatown, Thai Town, Little Ethiopia, and Little Tokyo show what a multilingual and cultural city Los Angeles is today. Mexicans comprise the largest ethnic group of Latinos in Los Angeles with 31.9% of the population, followed by Salvadorans (6%) and Guatemalans (3.6%). While the Latino population is spread throughout the city and its metropolitan area, it's most heavily concentrated in East Los Angeles, which has a very long established Central American and Mexican American community."[81]

However, while Los Angeles is a mini-United Nations, the city is anything but united.

---

80   *International Standard Bible Encyclopedia*, revised edition, © 1979 by Wm. Eerdmans Publishing Co. All rights reserved.
81   Los Angeles Population; 2019-08-28. Retrieved 2019-10-09 (see: http://worldpopulationreview.com/us-cities/los-angeles/ )

Jesus was saying that we start ministry at home. I believe the Lord has planted you in your city for the sake of the Kingdom. I believe there are people in your city that God wants to touch through your life, your testimony, your witness; people who your pastor would never be in a position to touch, even if they attended your church. God has placed *you* there on purpose. So be careful about the idea of "mission." You will be in danger of assuming that a mission is something you do when you go somewhere, when it more often than not is when you *are* somewhere. I have never met a successful pastor who did not love the city and people God assigned him.

One fact about racial division in our country is that racism is not new. Certainly, it appears that the schism between black and white gets all the press, but bigotry toward Latinos goes way back. In her article in the *Washington Post* in August 2019, Marie Arana put racism against Latinos into a broader historical perspective:

"These are long-held resentments. For centuries they have been fed by ignorance, racism and a stubborn unwillingness to understand a population whose ancestors were here by the millions—long before the first pilgrim set foot on Plymouth Rock. Now and then, the animus bubbles up. But bigotry against Hispanics has been an American constant since the Founding Fathers. Not 10 years after drafting the Declaration of Independence, Thomas Jefferson smugly suggested that these United States might want to snatch Latin America 'piece by piece.' John Adams held that a revolution in South America 'would be agreeable,' but he wanted little to do with 'a people more ignorant, more bigoted, more superstitious, more implicitly credulous in the sanctity of royalty, more blindly devoted to their priests … than any people in Europe, even in Spain'—managing to demonize a religion and dismiss a whole human order in one tweet-able and peevish rhetorical flourish."[82]

We have seen countless movies and documentaries about racist lynchings of black men and women in the South. However, we don't hear too much about such demonic treatment of Latinos. Lynchings of Hispanics became legion from California to Wyoming during those years too, yet they went ignored, tracked only by outraged Mexican diplomats who had little power to control the carnage.

As the early 20th century progressed, the volatile politics of our southern neighbor spurred even more Mexican emigration to the United States, delighting American businessmen who needed cheap labor to build railroad tracks, erect towns, toil on ranches and stoop over agricultural fields. Mexican Americans were wanted for their sweat, their military service, and their taxes, but not for their children or their company. As the United States forcefully expanded her borders south into formerly Mexican territory, creating what we now know as Texas, Arizona, New Mexico, Colorado, Utah, Nevada and California, that indigenous population had become a mestizo or mixed-race people. President William Taft crowed, "The whole hemisphere will be ours in fact as, by virtue of our superiority of race, it already is ours morally."[83]

Worthy of note is today's national climate created by loose-tongued rhetoric spewed across the airwaves. In a 2006 *New York Times* online article, without today's popularity of instant tweets and texts, using the old-fashioned microphone method and on national radio, New Jersey talk-show host Hal Turner exercised his constitutional right to voice his opinion, speaking of Latin America as a sinister, dark continent filled with "filthy, disease-ridden, two-legged bags of human debris...too stupid to believe.... Just think,

---

82  Arana, Marie; in an August 9, 2019, article in the *Washington Post* titled: "A History of anti-Hispanic bigotry in the United States."
83  See: https://www.nytimes.com/2019//03/02/us/porvenir-massacre-texas-mexicans.html

America, if we bring enough of them here, they can do for America exactly what they did for Mexico! Turn our whole country into a crime-ridden, drug-infested slum.... These people are subhuman. I would love it if folks who do have such weapons used them on the crowds.... I advocate machine-gunning these invaders to death at their rallies!" That diatribe from over a decade ago isn't a far cry from labels like "subhuman" and the Tweets of a certain president using descriptive words like "stupid," "filthy," "human debris," "rapists," "criminals," and "invasion" as slurs against Latinos. Yet, this terminology, in one form or another, has been in the American parlance for a very long time.[84]

## Each in its Own Proper Cultural Context

We live in a nation that has always been multi-racial and multi-cultural, a nation where racism is hundreds of years old. However, I don't think God is necessarily calling every church to be multi-racial or multi-cultural. I believe some of us live and worship in neighborhoods that are not racially or ethnically diverse, and that to strive for congregational diversity far beyond our immediate community might be an ecclesiastical stretch. On the other hand, for such congregations, the challenge may be to serve the Lord with the right mindset rather than a move. It might be teaching the ministry of reconciliation and how it might apply to those who work in different racial cultures more diverse than where they worship. For many of them, they will be the closest thing to the mind and love of Jesus in their work environment. That may be why God sent them there.

Take East St. Louis, Illinois, as an example. The town is somewhat like Nazareth in the Bible in that the question is often asked, "Can any good thing come out of E. St. Louis?" Many of

---

84  Ibid.

us loudly answer in the affirmative, including me, as well as such notable persons as tennis superstar Jimmy Connors, long jumper Jackie Joyner-Kersee and her husband Al Joyner, Major League Baseball player Hank Bauer, and others. Joe Mays, Miles Davis, the legendary Tina Turner and Ike Turner also had E. St. Louis addresses at one time.

Somewhere along the way, E. St. Louis picked up the nickname "East Boogie." I'm sure it was connected to the fact that the clubs and bars in St. Louis, across the river, closed at 2 am and the ones on our side of the river were open until 5 am. You could boogie almost all the way 'till sunrise. On my side of town, which was close to the bridges that crossed the Mississippi River, it was the all-night party place. The local black radio station KATZ had a disc jockey who came on at midnight. His show was called "Night Beat Down Rhythm Street," and he would broadcast live from a club called the Blue Note.

E. St. Louis is technically part of Greater St. Louis, Missouri. Separated by the Mississippi River, it was the "East Side" of metropolitan St. Louis. It's predominantly black. Jazz troubadour of another era, Lou Rawls, should have included St. Louis in his musical flight around America, pointing out that every major city has an "E. St. Louis" side. In his Live! album, "Southside Blues," his hit from that session, "Tobacco Road," zooms from city to city, stopping in the segregated side of Detroit, where they call it Black Bottom; Cleveland, where it's called Euclid Avenue and Central Avenue; Philadelphia, where it's known as South Street. In New York, it was Harlem. In Atlanta, it was Butter Bottom. In San Francisco, Fillmore. In Chicago, the South Side. And in Los Angeles you could find us in Watts and Compton. Every major city has a little E. St. Louis side.

The demographics of the city give you an interesting look at a small Midwest town: the median income for households in East

St. Louis, Illinois, is $20,659 (which breaks down to around $10 per hour), while the mean household income is $32,763. According to the most recent statistics, the racial composition was 95.65% black or African American and 1.91% white.[85] When I lived there, the city was significantly divided, with State Street being the main dividing line. My wife's family was one of the first black families to live on the "other side" of State Street. I don't know how many white people there were, but I lived in the South End, the all black neighborhood. Every church in our neighborhood was all black.

I never went to a white church until I enrolled in the University of Illinois. One Sunday, I attended the University Baptist Church. Now that I think about it, no one spoke to me at that church either. I later become organist at Salem Baptist Church in the black neighborhood in Champaign, Illinois. It was all black. Here's where I'm going with all this: I don't think either of these churches was called to be interracial or multi-cultural. Occasionally, white folk, usually students or faculty from U of I, would visit the church in Champaign. But my point is that I believe Kingdom work begins in your own community, your own Jerusalem. If that neighborhood, that community is multi-racial, I believe there should be an intentionality in reaching those beyond your own race, ethnicity, or culture.

From what I learned from Dr. E. K. Bailey, a principle emerged: the practice of Biblical theology is shaped by contextual reality. Put another way, the way you practice Biblical truth is shaped by your cultural context. How we worship, how we "work out our salvation" (Philippians 2:12) is directly related to the cultural context in which you do the working out.

The more you travel or study or watch the church in other cultures, the more you see ties that bind us woven within the fabric of the culture that is manifesting and preserving unique and

---

85 "World Population Review"; source: http://worldpopulationreview.com/us-cities/east-st-louis-il-population/

distinct elements of the context of the Christian life. There are non-negotiables shrouded with the flexibility of the parts of that particular culture. For example, there will be prayer, there will be Scripture reading in some form or another, there will be singing, and there will be the declaration of the Word of God.

However, the prayers are in another language, and the Scriptures may be extended passages or a repetition of just a few pages of the Bible, but those few pages may be the only Bible they have for their corporate gathering. The singing may be by a robed choir ensemble wearing jeans or by a spotlighted soloist. The preaching may be an exposition of a text, or the text may be a launching pad into an encouraging word delivered by a man or woman who may have letters behind their names or by a man or woman who has merely memorized and extemporized a text, passage, or thought inspired by a few words in the text. The illustrations and applications of the message are sometimes examples of biblical passages and scenes with appropriate related highlights or stories or tales or proverbs, or creations of the speaker that mirror elements of the personal or corporate lives of the worshipers.

To ignore or be unaware of the cultural values and cultural impressions on the minds of the hearers can be tragic and sometimes spiritually disastrous. God's people may be different from God's other people or groups or ethnicities, and they may approach worshiping and learning about Him in different ways from one another, but they all have a basic common thread and goal running through their services: dissemination of the love, the light, and the teaching of the Word of God.

I remember several years ago speaking at a small church in Soweto, South Africa, that met in the community room of a YMCA. They came three on a mule and were packed in that church like sardines. The room was set up with bleachers, but people were sitting on the floor and in the doorway, overflowing to allow those who had no seat to stand throughout the service.

I don't recall the message I gave, but I remember the illustration I tried to make.[86] I was talking about how God allows us to step up to the batter's box. We may not hit a home run, but we should at least get on base, which gives those following us a chance to earn more runs if they too get on base and someone finally hits a home run, allowing even more runs to be scored. I talked about the tragedy of being left on base because your comrade strikes out. The run that could have been scored was left on the base, and the inning would be over. I talked about things like knocking home runs, teamwork between the infield and the outfield, and the thrill of a home run.

When a message falls flat and misses the mark, in African American church culture we call that "flunking." You flunked. About half through my clearly thought out, passion-filled delivery, I could tell the people were not getting it, and I didn't know how to logically get out of the story. In fact, I had done that message before and used the same illustration and the word was powerful, memorable. I killed it (an African American phrase for doing a great job). However, this time I was flunking. And suddenly it struck me even before I finished preaching: I was in Soweto, South Africa. In South Africa, *there is no baseball!* There are cricket, soccer, and rugby! It was a horrible experience. My problem was that I did not properly exegete the context.

Whether the church is in Texas or Tijuana, Chicago or Chile, the mandate to be ministers of reconciliation knows no boundaries. And we may worship one way in America and a different way in Brazil. We worship the same God, but we practice our worship in *cultural* ways. We may worship one way in America and worship another way in South America. The practice of biblical truth varies or is different and is shaped by the culture in which we practice it because the practice of biblical theology is shaped by our contextual

---

86  People often remember the stories of application in a message more than the detailed alliterative outline and carefully researched exegesis of a text.

theology. Not only do we express our theology in social context, but our sociology shapes how we practice our theology.

Latino theology zeroes in on one of Paul's passages about reconciliation, found in Galatians chapter 3. Paul teaches us that reconciliation is dual: it's vertical and it is horizontal. We are reconciled vertically to God through Jesus Christ, and we are to be reconciled with others horizontally through the power of the Spirit of God.

Paul's theology sees racism as a sin of separation. He pictures this graphically in Ephesians 2:13-14: "But now in Christ Jesus you who once were far away have been brought near by the blood of Christ. For He Himself is our peace, who has made the two groups one and has destroyed the barrier, the dividing wall of hostility." We are separated from God by a barrier, a dividing wall of hostility. Paul sees the power of God as the power to bring down the wall. The purpose of bringing down the wall of separation is to unite us with Himself (v15) and unite us with one another in Him (v16). The falling of the wall produces a dual-dimensioned unity, both vertically and horizontally.

The contemporary gospel group Jars of Clay put it this way:

*We are one in the Spirit, we are one in the Lord*
*We are one in the Spirit, we are one in the Lord*
*And we pray that our unity will one day be restored*
*And they'll know we are Christians by our love, by our love*
*Yeah, they'll know we are Christians by our love*[87]

I believe at least one of the keys to Latino theology is Paul's phrase "in Christ." He says in Galatians 3:28, "there is no Jew, there is no Gentile, there is no slave, there is no free in Christ. There is no male, there is no female." Over 170 times Paul uses the phrase

---

87   Jars of Clay; "We Are One in the Spirit." See: www.LyricFind.com

"in Christ." It is one of his favorite phrases for describing our relationship with God. And here in Galatians, Paul says that all of us are sons and daughters and all of us are in Christ, but we are equal. That's very important. We are all in Christ, and *we are all one*. So, we are both individuals, and we are a collection of individuals. And in Christ we are all equal.

Most of the conversation about racism in this country focuses on the tension between the white community and the black community, quite possibly because of the ever-present residue of slavery in America. However, racism is also seen in the attitudes and actions between whites and Latinos and even between Latinos and blacks. An NBC News story about Latino racism recently stated,

> "Latinos—even those whose roots in this land stretch back to before the nation's origins—still face overt and subtle racism and discrimination. Hate crimes against them are rising, and they are underrepresented in film, in high-tech jobs and in the federal government workforce. And when they advocate for equal treatment and representation—or even when they just speak Spanish in public—they hear over and over that they need to assimilate."[88]

It seems that the response to Latino Americans by the dominant culture focuses more on assimilating them into the fabric of America and less on the actual factor that hinders their assimilation: racism.

On the one hand, there is the call to "fit in," yet on the other hand is the message, "Don't come in." African Americans and Latino Americans share this paradox. Although African Americans are not as much a part of the immigration debate, they're still

---

88  Gamboa, Suzanne; NBC News story titled, "Racism, not a lack of assimilation, is the real problem facing Latinos in America." Also see: https://www.nbcnews.com/news/latino/racism-not-lack-assimilation-real-problem-facing-latinos-america-n974021

receiving pushback against entrance and acceptance into some of the good-old boys clubs, while being told they're welcome. The so-called open doors often lead to closed rooms. The NBC story cites Ian Haney López, author of *Racism on Trial: The Chicano Fight for Justice*[89] and a law professor at the University of California:

> "There is an ingrained perception among many white people that all Latinos are foreign no matter how long they've been in the United States or how 'assimilated' they are.... Many whites view us as 'foreign' when measured against white people, both in terms of physical and cultural differences, and then collapse that into the assumption that we're foreign in the national sense as well.... The majority of Hispanics are born in the U.S., and Latino immigration has been declining markedly in the last decade. Yet some Hispanics whose family roots in America date back centuries are still asked, especially if they have dark skin, where their family is from."[90]

Racism is a coat of many colors. It is a chameleon shrouded in the fashion of the moment. It can change hues. It's a spin master. It is skilled in camouflage. Indiana University political science professor Bernard Fraga, author of *The Turnout Gap: Race, Ethnicity and Political Inequality in a Diversifying America*, describes it as a "push and pull" for Latinos who are told that to get more rights, they have to assimilate. Fraga says, "Assimilate is the excuse we use when opportunity is denied.[91]

---

89   See: https://www.amazon.com/Racism-Trial-Chiacano-Fight-Justice/dp/0674016297

90   Gamboa, Suzanne; NBC News story titled, "Racism, not a lack of assimilation, is the real problem facing Latinos in America." Also see: https://www.nbcnews.com/news/latino/racism-not-lack-assimilation-real-problem-facing-latinos-america-n974021

91   Ibid.

The key to Latino theology is a word called "Mestizo."
*Mestizo* means "mixture;" that is, a person who is of mixed race.
In an InterVarsity article titled "3 Latino Lessons on Racial
Reconciliation," Steven Tamayo states:

> "Being Latino is, for many of us, an experience of being
> mixed. All jumbled up. Mestizo. Latinos came to be when
> continents collided. Africa crashed into Europe to create
> Spain and Portugal. Spain and Portugal smashed into
> the indigenous communities in the Americas and the
> Caribbean, bringing Africa with them through the practice
> of slavery. Bam! Latinos."[92]

Here's the important thing to understand about Mestizo:
it means *mixed*, yet each one is as equally affirmed and loved and
blessed by God as an individual as any other human being on the
planet. When the Bible says there is no Jew, no Greek, no slave, no
free, it means that they are all equal sons and daughters of God.
That's why you need to be careful with the concept of trying to be
colorblind. Being colorblind is not some sort of advantage because
we are all to be valued for who we are. God loves the black in me
and the German in me, and God loves the Filipino in me and the
Chinese in me, and He loves the Japanese in me and the Nigerian
in me and the African in me. And He loves the Mexican in me. No
one is better than the other. I realize this might drive some racists
even more crazy than they may already be, but *we are all the same*.

Mestizaje (a metaphor for Latin theology) includes a
theological dimension of mixture. Latino theology says God blesses
what the world rejects. The world rejects mixtures of cultures and
ethnicities, so one element of the issue of racism is intermarriage.
There is a fear of one race intermarrying with another.

---

92 Tamayo, Steven, in an February 22, 2013, article titled "3 Latino Lessons on Racial
Reconciliation"; InterVarsity. https://intervarsity.org/blog/3-latino-lessons-racial-reconciliation

On the other hand, there is a challenge within the ranks of the disenfranchised. It is a principle that goes back to Cain and Abel and Joseph and his brothers. Beyond the outward battle against dominant culture is the reality of in-fighting. I won't delve into all of the psychological and economic factors that play into this painful reality, but Latinos and African Americans both must face the conflicts of internecine "friendly" fire. Tamayo states:

> "Few people dislike Latinos more than other Latinos. This is our dirty little secret. The category 'Latino' lumps together a broad spectrum of countries, traditions, languages, and dialects. And we do not always get along. This is not unique to the Latino community, though, is it? I bet, if you look around, you can find tension within your own ethnic community. It's tempting to think of reconciliation as happening only across ethnic lines: White to Black, Asian to Latino, ad infinitum. But there are lines everywhere. And while the lines may be thicker between Latinos and non-Latinos, the thin lines between Cubans and Chicanos still prove significant. Crossing these lines is a significant act of reconciliation."[93]

One of the front-line activists in Los Angeles for the past 20 or more years has been Najee Ali. In commenting on the Black Lives Matter movement, Ali makes this observation:

> "...When an African American murders another in our community, we're also at the forefront of these issues, as well, with our allies in the gang intervention and peace movement aiding and consoling grieving family members, holding vigils, peace marches and whatever else we can do to

---

93   Ibid.

help bring peace in our hood. That's what separates us from the #BlackLivesMatter movement in L.A. BLM only comes out when a White cop kills a Black person in a controversial shooting —which, on average is twice a year, at best —while dozens of Black folks are murdered by another Black folk, annually."[94]

The often vicious disputes and the devaluing of life by brothers and sisters of the same group seem to be an equal opportunity employer that is prevalent among all strata of our divided society.

When I read Scripture, I always look for myself in the text. Sometimes I see myself in a story of victory and power and provision. Other times I see myself in the stories of failure and faithlessness and weakness. Most often I want to see how closely the character is a reflection of me. One of the greatest blessings I have ever received from the Word of God is the truth that there are people in there who not only triumph like I do, who not only fail like I do, but who also look like I do.

When I was a kid, my sister would get dolls for Christmas. As I think back to those formative days, I recall that all of her dolls had blond hair and often blue eyes and always white skin. Later in life I would identify how such imaging impacted and helped shape my worldview—a view that placed value and worth on faces of a hue that was not like me. My sister had a room full of dolls that did not look like her. Not one looked like her. I guess back then the decision makers and designers at the big U.S. toy companies categorized black dolls as an unnecessary anathema.

But I do recall the great media event marking the first black doll to finally hit the American market. I remember because a dear friend of mine, Howard Neal, named his daughter after the company: Shindana.

---

94   *Compton Herald;* an August 25, 2015, article titled "Black-on-Black crime: all Black lives matter."

"A 13-inch black doll named Baby Nancy made her American Toy Fair debut, which took place the week of March 2, 1969.... Baby Nancy made her debut at the American Toy Fair. A 13-inch black baby doll, Nancy transformed what was racially acceptable in Toyland.... The revolutionary doll's manufacturer was a newcomer to the trade: Shindana Toys. Nancy was its maiden doll, a product of the rebirth of Los Angeles after the 1965 Watts rebellion. That October, two months after the riots, Robert Hall and Louis Smith, two black civil rights activists working in Watts, founded Operation Bootstrap, Inc.—a not-for-profit community development and job training center dedicated to the Black Power movement."[95]

For the first time, little black girls could hold dolls in their hands that looked like them with hair, lips and skin color like theirs. When we look at the variety of doll toys available now, we can't imagine not having the option. But it wasn't always that way.

## Mixed, Yet One

As significant as it is to see yourself in the face of a doll, it is equally important that each of us sees ourselves in the God story.

The practice of Biblical theology is shaped by contextual reality. Your theology is shaped by the context in which you do theology. Your interpretation of theology is based on your understanding of your culture. For example, Latino theology sees Latinos in the Scriptures. There are many things that we can learn from Latino theology, because it is based on the concept of being mixed or a mixture since when Mestizo tribes or areas were conquered by the Spanish, they were conquered to be oppressed. That is, until somebody

---

95   Goldberg, Rob, in a March 12, 2019, *Los Angeles Times* Op-Ed titled "Baby Nancy, the first 'black' doll, woke the toy industry."

started reading the Bible because God blesses what the world rejects. They learned that Jesus was mixed, that He had four Gentile women in His bloodline who were of a different race.

Having been a grown man before I saw that there are black people in the Bible, I know what it feels like to see yourself in God's plan. Mestizaje, or Latino theology, says we are mixed, just as Jesus was mixed. Latino theology says that Latino people are a mixture of different cultures, races, and languages. This is because, historically, most Latinos have bloodlines from Europeans, from Africans, from Asians, and from American Indians. There is literally no single bloodline in a Latino or Hispanic man or woman. Latino theology says it is because we were mixed that we didn't fit into the culture, we were marginalized, set aside. Yet we are one with the Almighty God, and through His Son—who also was a mixed man with Gentile blood running through His veins—we are one with His body the Church. To be a Mestizo and see the principle of oneness with Almighty God through Jesus Christ allows a Mestizo to see the power of God and the power of blessed mixture.

Latin theology provides a race conscious foundation for individual and group identity that transcends culture, race and socioeconomic status. It is the power of God and one's blessed identity in Him that eclipses and replaces all relationships with mutual affirmation and value. Hispanics can share a common language and hybrid cultures, yet not be a single race. Blends of European, American Indian, African and Arabic ancestors are likened to the art of the apothecary that mixes ingredients to produce a blessed divine diversity in unity that cannot condone social stratification and domination.

Racism is, by definition, a sin before the God who unifies. This unifying God sent His Son Jesus as a messianic mestizaje, marginalized into a culture of the disinherited, the outcast, and the downcast. He became the Messiah of the marginalized. Thus, racism moves you to the margins only to find a marginalized Messiah who greets you with unifying love. Those afar off, marginalized on the fringes of society, are brought into oneness with the God whose Son meets them there. There was no room for Him either, in the sheltered inns of society. As a Galilean, Jesus was among the marginalized, from the wrong side of the tracks, but it is there in the margins of society that Jesus comes both as one also marginalized and as one who is liberator to bring all people out with dignity and value by His power.

The mestizaje dimension of the life of Christ, mixed blood, mixed ethnicity, and mixed culture was the very basis of His salvific assignment. He belonged to more than one culture but was not fully engulfed in either.

As a citizen of Jerusalem, Jesus was consecrated and condemned at the culmination of His self-sacrificing public ministry. From the ghetto of Galilee, He chooses to enter the "big city" of Jerusalem, to suffer the oppression and bigotry in the middle of the very culture He would challenge. He enters as a mixed Galilean and is drawn to the down-and-outs, bringing comfort in their oppression but enabling them to confront and transcend and transform the very society that rejected Him. He chose the mixed side of Himself; He came to seek and to save those who were lost in the margins of sin and social segregation. He brought dignity. He brought equality. He brought unity.

Latino/Mestizaje are terms also imposed by the U.S. Census Bureau to identify immigrants that don't fit into the dichotomy of a predominantly biracial black and white America.[96] The problem

---

96  The U.S. Office of Management and Budget (OMB) requires federal agencies to use a minimum of two ethnicities in collecting and reporting data: Hispanic or Latino and Not Hispanic or Latino. OMB defines "Hispanic or Latino" as a person of Cuban, Mexican, Puerto Rican, South or Central American, or other Spanish culture or origin regardless of race. People who identify with the terms "Hispanic" or "Latino" are those who classify themselves in one of the specific Hispanic or Latino categories listed on the decennial census questionnaire and various Census Bureau survey questionnaires—"Mexican, Mexican Am., Chicano" or "Puerto Rican" or "Cuban"—as well as those who indicate that they are "another Hispanic, Latino, or Spanish origin." See: https://www.census.gov/topics/population/hispanic-origin/about.html

is that many, if not most, of these immigrants don't fit all the way into either category. Isn't that like Jesus? He was the God-Man. Too much God to be all man, and too much man to be all God; yet, He was neither—and He was both: All God and All Man.

And it is the power of this God-Man Jesus, God of unity, who causes walls of separation to fall no matter what one's theology or interpretation of Galatians 3:28-29 may be: "There is neither Jew nor Greek, there is neither slave nor free, there is neither male nor female, for you are all one in Christ Jesus. If you belong to Christ, then you are Abraham's seed, and heirs according to the promise."

Those two verses alone should settle the matter of the separation of peoples from one another once and for all.

# 7
# A SWING—AND A MISS?

*"Black power...is a call for black people in this country to unite,*
*to recognize that heritage, to build a sense of community.*
*It is a call for black people to begin to define their own goals,*
*to lead their own organizations and to support those*
*organizations. It is a call to reject the racist institutions*
*and values of this society."*
**—Charles Hamilton,** *Black Power!*[97]

Every black face caught in the Union building that night went
straight to jail. Including me.

I didn't learn why I had been crammed into the paddy wagon
until a few guys began quietly, urgently reviewing how they had pushed
past the unguarded main entrance after hearing about the killing of
Dr. King and soon realized that someone had already called the police.

That meant I just happened to be at the right place when the
wrong crowd showed up, followed by the police and dogs and guns
and barred vans. Which meant that the only time I had been in
jail in my life was an unplanned happenstance. I was an accidental
revolutionary, just trying to get to a party with my girl.

In future years, my mind would push the rewind button over
and over, taking me back to that night in the slammer while the
nation was in turmoil, teetering on the razor edge of racism, revenge
and riots. Occasionally, thinking back, I would wonder about the
people who had actually strategically planned that revolutionary
action. Because, although each of us students was on the precipice of

---

97   Hamilton, Charles; *Black Power!* (1967).

*treading into different lives ahead, we had four things in common that night: we were all fellow college students, we were all around the same age, we were all in jail together, and we were all black.* What became of their lives? *I would wonder.*

*Would they be as convicted as I would be?*

\* \* \*

There was a juggler who used to come on TV who had a unique juggling style. He would juggle balls and rings and bowling pins much like other jugglers, but the hook to his act was that he would put a hat on his head, and as he juggled, he would alternately put the hat on and take it off, on and off, all while continuing to juggle the bowling pins and rings or balls. He was a busy guy.

I often see myself in this guy's juggling act. Juggling one thing after another, all the while changing hats. I wear the hat of a flawed, failing child of God, trying to live out the love of my Lord and Savior. I wear the hat of a black man living in the fog of a society where lines of power and access are often tinted in skin color. I wear the hat of a father, trying to set a positive example for my children and grandchildren, an example fleshed out under the Lordship of the God I've given my life to. I wear the hat of a student with a passionate unquenchable hunger and thirst for the righteousness revealed in the Word of my God. I wear the hat of a teacher praying to be a channel of revelation and knowledge. I wear the hat of a pastor/preacher assigned the awesome task of leading sheep who often don't want to be led, helping people who often don't want to be helped, and answering the question "What must I do to be saved?" asked by people who don't want to be saved.

I'm like that juggler, constantly changing hats while constantly juggling my myriad responsibilities. Cue the calliope, and put me on a unicycle.

I hear the Lord declaring me an ambassador of Christ as an agent of reconciliation from 2 Corinthians 5:20, but I don't always know how to do that. I don't always know what that looks like. I feel so inadequate. I'm swapping hats while I write this piece. I don't want to come off as if I'm spouting indisputable *thus sayeth the Lord*-isms from the heights of ex cathedra. I don't want to invite you into the didactic climate of the theological classroom (*boring!*). I don't want to mount the sacred soapbox of the pulpiteer and spew preachments of exhortation or rebuke (*more* boring!). I certainly don't want to come off like the wise old father or grandfather, spinning tales of "Well, Sonny, back in my day..." (I started dozing off just typing those words!).

No, this issue is too serious to shroud it in lightweight banter. Yet, it's also too practical to weigh down with statistics, technical jargon, and platitudes of sanctity. I'm sure one of my hats will give me the tools and the traction to fulfill God's call on my life. I just don't know which one to wear at any given time or how to stack them all on my head at once. I add a voice into the discussion. I submit what I have received. I release it to you. But I have far more questions than answers.

In a nutshell, I see pieces of the puzzle, but I don't always know how to put them together. And I can't throw my hands up and run from the battle just because there's no assurance of victory. That would ignore the necessary element of faith. Without faith—regardless of what we know or do—we can't possibly please God says Hebrews 11:6. For me, this is a real-life existential struggle. I wrestle with it. I try to reason with it. I fight for it—without fully understanding what a "win" would look like.

It is a conundrum, this business, this joy, this honor, this blessing, of being a child of God—who bestowed on me an anointing to lead and to teach. Where do I even start?!

A good place to start is to look up. Lift up my eyes beyond the obstacles and walls and hills and challenges and divisions that stand before me and declare humbly and with a measure of resignation, "Lord, I need your help!" (Psalm 121)

The first revelation I see is that whatever this idea of reconciliation looks like, it begins with the Lord. He is always the one to make the first move. A theology of reconciliation is birthed out of a context of fractured relationships, division, separation, enmity, estrangement. It assumes the need to fill the gap. God has made the first move. The next move is ours. The ball is in our court. We are called to move toward Him and fill that gap.

This issue of reconciliation is multidimensional. First of all, reconciliation is an ongoing process. It's a process that involves forgiveness. It involves repentance. It involves justice. It involves restoration. It is not a quick fix. As important as it is, it is not merely about a law being passed. It is more than a march or a rally. It is more than turning a page of history assuming that the case closed with the turning of the historical page.

That's why it is often offensive when the question is raised, "Why can't you people get past that?" "That was yesterday; those days are gone." "GET OVER IT!" If I step on your foot, I can't tell you when it stops hurting. Especially if you're still standing on it. On the other hand, we must acknowledge and affirm the value of forward steps along the journey. Steps have been made. Good steps. Some giant steps. Some baby steps. But steps, nonetheless.

\* \* \*

In 1996, I stood on the grass backstage at the Oakland Coliseum as the pulsing rhythms of the praise team and band concluded their musical declarations of the love of God. The stadium was jam-packed with 40,000 men that felt, looked and sounded like twice that many. As I nervously waited to be called onto the stage to be introduced to address this august crowd, for the only time in my life, my knees buckled, gave way and I slid down to the green grass at my feet. I could hear in my spirit the voice of my mother, "Look at God!" I remember trembling at the thought of preparing to address a stadium full of spiritually hungry men. Zipping through my mind in a whisper, as if on a loop, I heard, *This is a long way from E. St. Louis!*

It was the second Promise Keepers event. I was a speaker. One of my spiritual fathers, Dr. E. V. Hill, a nationally acclaimed preacher of the gospel, spoke at the first PK event in Denver and had a hand in getting me invited as one of the black speakers on the roster.

In the ensuing years, I would stand in some of the largest stadiums in the nation, places like the Orange Bowl and the Los Angeles Coliseum, each packed wall-to-wall with men. I would often ponder how and why the Lord allowed me to be part of such a majestic movement. I would stand alongside men who were or would become giants in my eyes and many who would become dear friends.

Several things stick in my memory from my days in Promise Keepers, which I deem to be a top-down approach to the issue of racism. (We'll take a look at that, as well as the alternate strategy: bottom up.) Having been part of the movement for most of its years, I think I have a perspective that might be clearer than many of the guys in the stands. I was one of them and proud to be so. Every year, we would receive a list of dates and stadiums which would host the PK events for the next year. We were allowed to choose as many as ten dates per tour. This was a calendar priority for me, and I would annually commit to between seven and nine events, often shuffling my schedule to make it work.

The first thing I noticed was that there were always only a few of us black participants. I met and would often see Tony Evans (who became a dear friend to this day) and Crawford Loritts (not only a lifelong friend, but whose son is my godson). As well as guys like

Raleigh Washington out of Chicago, who was in the inner circle of top leadership, Dr. John Perkins, the living legend and civil rights general. Great men. But very few of us.

The second thing I noticed was that there weren't very many faces of color in the stands, either. In fact, it's safe to say that in most gatherings there were more brown Latino faces than black African American faces. So, let me drop this in right here: one of the challenges of experiencing the grace of God in opening doors for your life and giving you a place to stand in unusual or unfamiliar places is *pride*. I have had to ask for forgiveness when I have risen up in arrogance or pride or a carnal sense of favoritism. I have been in "small" circles of dark faces who didn't really care whether the room granted entry to other dark faces or not.

On the other hand, the flipside of ungodly arrogance was the value I placed on being in the room at all, no matter who else was or wasn't there. In other words, I felt I was there to represent what I knew was a key plank in the platform of the movement: breaking down the walls of racism that at least everyone there acknowledged was a blight on society. One of the promises of a Promise Keeper was to stand against racism in our country. When a man signed up to be a Promise Keeper, he made a commitment to reach beyond racial barriers and be an expression of the power of oneness, the power of godly unity, and a demonstration of the prayer of Jesus for His followers to be "one" (John 17:21). I believed I was there for that reason, if for no other.

Possibly the most profound thing I learned was that all of us men of color on the speakers lineup had a significantly right-leaning, conservative bent. The more I got to know the members of our small Sacro-frat, the more I realized that we all held theologically, sociologically, philosophically and politically conservative worldviews. I admit, I can be a slow learner sometimes, because it took me a while to see this glaring truth. Upon my enlightenment,

I wondered what took me so long to wake up and realize this common ground among us. It was hidden in plain sight.

I admit that I never truly digested the PK theological framework for the doctrinal statement, which I'm sure I would have had to sign somewhere along the way. But the more I looked around backstage and out over the audience in the stadium, I was more and more aware of the values and principles that covered the space.

Back to Oakland, '96. I didn't know that not only was the Coliseum gathering negligibly supported by the smattering of hued faces in the crowd, but there was a concerted move against the meeting by the African American church community in the Bay Area. The movement was tagged as sexist, homophobic, and an offspring born from the womb of the religious right. Aside from PK's anti-gay position, almost never attacked directly but clearly referenced in proclamations of men strengthening their marriages and being the men God has called them to be to the women they are married to, it clearly implied the unacceptable union of man and husband. It was a plank of the PK movement and was certainly biblical, but it was overtly strident, sometimes to the point of overshadowing many more urgent tenets of the Bible, including how we are to treat our fellow human beings—*all* of whom are God's children.

The tepid PK flag of racial unity did not present sufficient bait to reel in the whale-sized minority population of the host city. It was seen by some as a more sophisticated redress of attempts to simplistically address the complex elements of systemic institutional racism. The assumption of ineffectiveness seemed to erect another wall that would not fall the under the theme "Break Down the Walls." Certainly, these critiques did not stop the movement for almost a decade, but having been on stage after stage, I look back and wonder how much farther down the field we really kicked the can of racism out of the game of life.

Promise Keepers' founder, former University of Colorado

football coach Bill McCartney, affirmed the priority of breaking down racial boundaries when he said, "We're going to spend all eternity together. When we get up there, we want to be able to testify that we did it together.... Our destination is brotherhood in concert—true biblical oneness."[98]

I saw value in starting on the other side of the racism equation. I did not feel there was any conflict between the ultimate similar goals of the right or left flank of soldiers of the cross. I saw this as a God-honoring, Kingdom-driven attack on one of the securest and highest strongholds of the enemy. Yet, in terms of the effectiveness of achieving the goal of impacting the reality of racism, I fear the chasm between the extremes of our polarized culture was only bridged by glacial movement.

I did not agree with the critics who saw it as a ploy by the theological conservative camp of the body of Christ to, at best, put a multi-colored band-aid on the cancer of the sin of racism. I enlisted in this itinerate movement, which unashamedly put racism in its crosshairs as an enemy of the Kingdom of God. I gave Coach an Amen when he declared: "They are going to be able to say, 'Yes, we teach, preach, model and live racial reconciliation.' And when that happens, the church of Jesus Christ is going to be able to stand up and say we can testify that the giant of racism is dead inside the church of Jesus Christ."[99]

Author Gordon Dalbey, former pastor of United Church of Christ in the Los Angeles area, wrote one of the first books to address spiritual and emotional healing in men from a Christian standpoint and was a supporter of Promise Keepers. Dalbey commended it as excellent and a first-level opportunity for men to confront the truth about themselves. But also Dalbey stated that he felt the atmosphere of the gatherings didn't go far enough. He

---

98  CNN Interactive. "Promise Keepers fill Washington's Mall with prayer," October 4, 1997. Web posted at: 9:10 p.m. EDT (0110 GMT). http://www.cnn.com/US/9710/04/promise. keepers.pm/
99  Ibid.

said, "Promise Keepers is raising the behavior standards, which is marvelous to see. The next move has to be a deeper healing, a reliance on the grace of God in the face of inadequacy. I'd like to see less exhortation."[100]

I don't doubt the validity of that goal nor the sincerity of the recruits. One of the balls that were dropped, however, was the follow-up connection by local churches after those of us on the PK stage packed up and moved on to the next stadium. It was encouraging to see the interdenominational, even interreligious (albeit on a small scale) support and participation the movement received. But I am not so sure there was retention of male involvement in the local churches, or at least whether or not there was sufficient accurate measurement of the results. And, though we encouraged the men to align or re-align with a local congregation, I really don't know how many churches had an appreciable ongoing increase in male involvement.

We would often see men weeping at the altar in response to a call to confess or forgive marital failures and/or covenant to live in practical spiritual, moral, ethical, and sexual purity. But, again, I don't think we established a sufficient network of follow-up support—particularly for the men who were not in and did not commit to a local church family. Certainly, we can take the spiritual highground and say, "We leave the results to God and trust the Holy Spirit," but I don't think we really knew how well the movement did in achieving its goals.

On the other hand, some of the left-leaning nay-sayers on the sidelines would suggest that it was the very emphasis on the supernatural dynamic of the movement that doomed it from the beginning. As one critic wrote in a Christian magazine:

100   Dart, John, Times Staff Writer. 'Promise Keepers,' a Message to L.A. Men: Conference: Gathering at the Coliseum includes 15 hours of events designed to spread the group's belief in traditional father-husband duties. About 70,000 are expected to attend. Los Angeles Times. May 6, 1995.

"The PK leaders contend for a supernatural operation of the Holy Spirit—when no such experience is available today. While miraculous revelation and signs were a part of the apostolic experience in the first century, those wonders were removed from the church's possession when the New Testament canon was completed (1 Corinthians 13:8-10). Today, there is not one fact that anyone knows about the character of God, the life and work of Jesus Christ, the gospel, or what God's will for man is, except that which is learned from the Bible. No person has ever been discovered in any remote region of the earth who knows anything of these matters, if he has been totally isolated from the influence of the written Word."[101]

I cite this critique only to highlight the kind of expected opposition faced by the sincere motives of a movement that had a good run, but as several challenges became more and more obvious, like a TV drama that lasted several seasons, PK ultimately lost its audience.

I was a member of the "cast" at many events; not one of the "producers" or in the inner-circle of Promise Keepers decision makers, and cannot claim to have been in the know about the inner workings of the organization. My first hint that something was significantly changing was when I received the annual letter announcing the dates and venues for the upcoming year. I immediately noticed that the massive football stadiums in major markets we had once booked had been replaced by far smaller venues such as college stadiums as well as basketball arenas. The last events I did were in Rochester, New York, San Diego, and the American Airlines Arena in Dallas. The Dallas event arena was

---

101   Jackson, Wayne. "What's Wrong with the Promise Keepers Movement?" ChristianCourier.com. Access date: October 11, 2019. https://www.christiancourier.com/articles/110-whats-wrong-with-the-promise-keepers-movement

filled but lacked the excitement and anticipation of the attendees at the Oakland Coliseum.

I believe the providential timing that placed our efforts in a time of hunger and spiritual thirst among men was running parallel to a culture, a nation, a society that was becoming even more secular and humanistic. By the time PK had crisscrossed the nation, there was a more subtle non-religious wave creeping across the country. Noting the impact on the Catholic church attendance in a New England town (considered a bastion of left-leaning liberalism), church observers noted what would be justifiably applicable beyond the ranks of Catholicism:

> "Catholicism was more prevalent in Portsmouth in the 1980s, but church attendance began to decrease in the late 1990s, leading to the three churches joining under one parish in 2006. 'Shifts in the city's demographics played a part in this,' he said, 'but secularism was a factor.'"[102]

Aside from the equally weighted activism for gender equality and gay rights, the left more aggressively and more deliberately picked up the mantle of fighting racism. The theo-philosophical package of the conservative goals of racial equality had been overshadowed by the more acceptable, more palatable, more popular left and alt-right prophets and prophetesses whose followers could take the same journey and arrive at the same land of equality without the baggage of theological exclusivism. It seems the church was losing the battle against racism to secular, pseudo-spiritual mindsets that wanted to win the battle against the same enemy.

---

102   *Crux*, "Losing our religion: The rise of secularism on the Seacoast"; https://cruxnow. com/church-in-the-usa/2017/02/27/losing-religion-rise-secularism-seacoast/ Associated Press. Feb 27, 2017

## A God of Seasons

My greatest takeaway from the PK era is that God is a God of seasons. In my 71 years on this earth, I have learned the truth of the rock group The Byrds. The whose words of the lingering tune that flowed regularly from the jukebox of the campus hangout at the U of I were a 1965 cover of Solomon's ancient prophetic words from Ecclesiastes 3:1.

> *To everything (turn, turn, turn)*
> *There is a season (turn, turn, turn)*
> *And a time to every purpose, under heaven*

God is a God of seasons. I have seen seasons of conservatives vs. liberals, mainline churches vs. evangelical churches, tongue talkers vs. non-tongue talkers, oneness vs. Trinitarians, and women can preach vs. woman can't even speak in church, to everything in between (turn, turn, turn). I have seen the church in historical vicissitudes from within and without. I have seen the church rise in victory, again and again. To everything (turn, turn turn).

The season of mass stadium events as a strategy for fighting racism came and went. But there is a tension of principles God sovereignly providentially chooses when a season is in transition. Sometimes He changes wineskins, preparing new wine for old wineskins. Sometimes He does a "new" thing for a different time— an updated version of last season's model. From Saul to Paul. From Abram to Abraham. Sara to Sarai. Simon to Peter.

But sometimes He does a whole new thing. Not just new wine in old wineskins, but new wine for new wineskins. Because some new wine won't fit in the old wineskins. And when He does a new thing, something new in kind, it is something brand new, a new creation.

God says in Isaiah, "Behold I am doing a new thing." *The Message* paraphrase captures the essence of this "new" thing, in Isaiah 43:19. "Be alert, be present. I'm about to do something brand-new. It's bursting out! Don't you see it?" The word for "new" means something not done before. It is not so much a remodeling or update of what has been done in the past, it is new as in fresh and not seen before.

But here's the challenge: when God does a new thing, new in kind, a brand new creation, the new person in Christ *looks the same on the outside*. I believe the new Promise Keepers will be more than a revised update of what they did in the '90s. It will be an opportunity for God to do something different and new that demonstrates what Paul paraphrased when he said, "Your eyes have not seen [this new thing], your ears have not heard." (1 Corinthians 2:9) I pray it will be something new as a demonstration of racial harmony and unity. I pray it will launch a season in answer to the prayer of Jesus, "That they may be one." (John 17:21)

PK is in a new season. Some things will look like the old season. Some things will be brand new. Some things will look the same on the outside, but they will be driven by a new engine, new technology, new structures, new drive train. The key is, we won't know what the new season will be like until they get into it, until it gets rolling, road tested, and out there to the "public."

God never puts all of His eggs in one basket. Even when we seem to swing and miss, He always aims to get the glory while moving us forward into new seasons in the direction of His ultimate goal: that everyone be *one* in Him.

# 8
# TUG OF WAR

*"We will never fully understand how far we've come as a nation until we accept and acknowledge the spectacular abominations that passed as normal. Do not trifle with this history. Not unless you are willing to understand the meaning, the weight, the horror, the ardor, the hatred, the stain, the special brand of evil associated with it...."*
—**Michele Norris,** former Host of "All Things Considered," National Public Radio[103]

*It would be awhile after the frightening incident at the University of Illinois Student Union that I would become convicted— albeit by a jazz/folk song. A song that over the years would occasionally thrust me into a chasm of regret over having gotten my street/jail/ revolution cred by pure happenstance that violent night:*

> *You will not be able to stay home, brother*
> *You will not be able to plug in, turn on and drop out*
> *You will not be able to lose yourself on skag and*
> *Skip out for beer during commercials*
> *Because the revolution will not be televised*
> *The revolution will not be televised*
> *The revolution will not be right back after a message*
> *About a white tornado, white lightning, or white people*

103   Norris, Michele; former host of NPR's "All Things Considered" and Founding Director of the Race Card Project; in an October 23, 2019, article in the *Washington Post* titled "So you want to talk about lynching? Understand this first." See: https://www. washingtonpost.com/opinions/so-you-want-to-talk-about-lynching-understand-this-first/2019/10/23/c5a5fd2a-f5ae-11e9-ad8b-85e2aa00b5ce_story.html

*You will not have to worry about a germ in your bedroom*
*a tiger in your tank, or the giant in your toilet bowl*
*The revolution will not go better with Coke*
*The revolution will not fight the germs that cause bad breath*
*The revolution WILL put you in the driver's seat*
*The revolution will not be televised*
    *WILL not be televised, WILL NOT BE*
*TELEVISED*
    *The revolution will be no re-run, brothers*
*The revolution will be live*[104]

\* \* \*

Far too often I have gone through a season of push and pull, an inner tug of war. Sometimes it's brief and fleeting, sometimes lingering, depending on my physical location. I have trudged through clouds of tension between the blackness in my face and the Bible in my hand. This tug and pull has sometimes frustrated me and often angered me. *Why am I trippin'?* Am I going through this, or am I *putting* myself through it? Or are others putting me through it?

It flares up in some of the circles I run in. It flares up in some platforms where I have stood. It raises its head very often during political seasons. Maybe it is in the face of shifting political change that the opposing tug and pull becomes more and more taut.

I can't express the excitement, the joy and the thrill I experienced as I stood on the Mall of Washington D.C., with my wife, my son, and my daughter and her son. In the 20-odd degree Fahrenheit weather, I strained to quickly wipe away the tears that crept out of the corners of my eyes before they froze. I laughed to myself a few times at the irony of being in this festive, frigid

---

104  Source: Lyric Find. Songwriters: Gil Scott-Heron. The Revolution Will Not Be Televised lyrics © Warner Chappell Music, Inc.

crowd, celebrating the first black man to soon move into the White House.[105] It almost sounded like an oxymoron: *Black Man/White House*. My mind was spinning.

The inexpressible pride I felt hearing Aretha Franklin sing, gave me flashbacks of the great gospel queen, Mahalia Jackson, singing on the same mall years before at the Civil Rights March led by her friend, Dr. Martin Luther King, Jr. Now in the cold winds sweeping across the Mall, the Queen of Soul stands where the Queen of Gospel stood. I was amazed at the massive crowd navigating through the streets. I had never been in a gathering of that many predominantly black faces in my life.

Years later I would chuckle about the debate (lackluster as it was for most of America with access to a television) over whether Obama had a larger crowd at his inauguration than Donald Trump at his. I think that was the first indication to me that what comes out of the mouth of the present occupant of that same White House cannot always be trusted, nor can he be expected to speak with veracity.

Flashback. 1984. Election time. The spotlight is on the Reverend Jesse Jackson, a black man running for the White House. It was a time of inner turmoil for me on several levels. I was keenly aware that there were philosophical differences between Dr. Jackson and myself. I felt a tension between the prominence of my blackness and the priority of my Bible. But this was the first time I felt the tugs in a political sense. This was real. I had met Jesse by then, but I didn't know him nearly as well as I would come to know him by the time he ran the second time. The black community was buzzing at

---

105    Contrary to a popular myth, the White House did not get its name because it was built and expected to only occupy white people. The building was first painted white to cover scorch marks left after British soldiers set fire to the house during the War of 1812. The White House was first coated in a lime-based whitewash in 1798 to protect the exterior stone from moisture and cracking during winter freezes. The term "White House" was occasionally used before the War of 1812, with the phrase appearing in newspapers in the first decade of the 19th century. President Theodore Roosevelt officially named the Executive Mansion the "White House" in 1901.

the possibility of a black man in charge at the White House. It was a time of black pride, and I felt it. It was a good feeling.

However, I had friends in the ministry, business, academic, and professional fields who could not understand why I was so thrilled over the candidacy of Jesse Jackson. He doesn't read his Bible the way I and many of my peers in the pulpit do. Jesse is far too liberal. Yet, he was my friend. And the tug tightened.

One of my mentors, the late, Dr. E. V. Hill, was one of the most acclaimed preachers—black or white—in the country. He was also a bold, unashamed, unapologetic black Republican. He once ran for presidency of the National Baptist Convention, U.S.A., the largest black organization in the world. Some say he lost because he was a staunch Republican. Dr. Hill was also a popular national TV minister and was known in some circles as pastor to Paul and Jan Crouch, owners of the very conservative national TV station, TBN. It was through Dr. Hill's national prominence that he had raised millions of dollars (mostly from white people) to support his ministry of feeding the hungry in central Los Angeles.

One day I was in Dr. Hill's office in the middle of Jesse Jackson's bid for the presidency. Dr. Hill, who had coined Jesse's campaign slogan "Run Jesse, Run," was slowly opening mail in front of his cluttered desk when he said something like, "Well, there goes a million."

I said, "A million what, Pop?"

"Today I lost a million dollars in support for The Lord's Kitchen," he replied.

He explained that since he had gone public in support of Jesse's run for the White House, he was getting letters from his conservative white donors telling him they were withdrawing their support of this feeding ministry. The loss had reached one million dollars.

I knew he had not changed his conservative theology or ideology, but I also knew his blackness had won the tug on him over his right-leaning theology and lost the tug on him for backing a left-leaning candidate.

A cold wind swept across my face that morning on the chilly National Mall at Barack Obama's inauguration, and my thoughts returned from the scene in Dr. Hill's office. Jesse didn't win his bid for the presidency, of course, but his valiant effort raised my black pride. Some of my white friends never understood how I, a conservative Christian, could feel that way.

My friendship with Jesse Jackson taught me to find comfort in the tension between my color and my convictions. Most of all, I value a friendship that transcends the walls of theological differences. Jesse Jackson is an extremely gifted preacher. He studied at a renowned liberal seminary, Chicago Theological Seminary, yet his preaching gift was heralded by right and left-leaning black churchmen and women alike.

One Sunday, Jesse preached at our church. I asked him not to make it a campaign or political event. I told him all I wanted was Jesus. We chuckled, but he got the point. Then he went on to preach one of the most powerful messages I've ever heard. I mean, that brother *preached the paint off the walls*.

In the office after the service, he asked me if I wanted to go with him to the Bay Area. I told him I couldn't make it but asked what the occasion was. He said it was an event for the support of the gay community.

I told him, "Man, you know I can't roll with you on that one."

It wasn't an issue of whether or not we agreed on the gay marriage issue. (We definitely didn't.) The point was that we both had learned to love and respect and value each other beyond our differences, refusing to allow walls of dissonance to separate the friendship.

Back to the chilly mall and President Obama, my mind searched way back to a civics report I did in high school on the

death of President John Kennedy in 1963. I shuddered in a brief grip
of fear that some deranged person might snuff out the life of the
object of this historical occasion hundreds of years in the making.
And the tug intensified.

As I stood shifting from one foot to the other, clutching hand
warmers that did nothing to dispel the bite in the January air, I
found myself repeating a prayer in my mind for this man who was
among the most popular men in the world. "Lord, protect this man.
Protect his family."

Over and over again. *Protect this man and his family.*

Again, I would feel the carnal tug in my mind that I was praying
for a man I admired about as much as I disagreed with him. The tug
of my sociological liberalism stretched to bring me back to center from
the pull of my theological conservatism. I felt myself pushing down
deeper into my theological roots, while bending in the liberal winds
that filled the air of the beautiful gathering that day.

I recalled the yarn that I had told so many times in the
pulpit about the talking palm tree that swayed in my front yard in
Los Angeles during a rare severe thunderstorm. That tree would
prophetically plead with me to be like the palm tree in the storm. *I
might bend, but I won't break.* Like the hypothetical palm tree whose
leaves waved in the wind, I joined in over and over again, with the
chilled crowd around me, waving, cheering, clapping, celebrating.
Bending but not breaking.

Like the hypothetical palm, bending but without hypocrisy, I
felt pride in the moment that sent my mind back to seeing my mother
clean the houses and toilets of white people to send me to college,
hearing my daddy called *nigga* by a white cop while I held my dad's
hand and looked up into his embarrassed but staunch face—but
without hypocrisy, because I remembered the prohibiting signs of
"White only" or "White fountain" that were part of my family's
annual vacations to the South and some places in the North. Without

hypocrisy because I remembered the high school counselor who told me I couldn't make it at the University of Illinois (partially because he said it was too big, but certainly because I would be a member of the sparse black student body). The truth is, I was blowing in the historical winds of political change (even progress) in honor of a man I was so proud of, ethnically, but so far from, theologically.

As I stood on the historic grassy area with my family, the wind blew my mind back to a conversation I had with a dear friend just days after President Obama announced his candidacy. I was in the green room of national Christian TV station TBN, waiting to go on set to promote my latest book, and to my surprise, a dear friend of mine was also there, promoting his book.

I asked him how he felt about Senator Obama's announcement.

He shrugged in exasperation and said something along the lines of, "I told Barack to stay as far away from me as he could."

*Ouch.*

"Man, you know that's not going to happen," I responded. "You know when the press gets wind of this, they're going to eat him up."

He agreed and said he had told Obama that the run was going to hurt him. We both knew it was only a matter of time.

That man was my friend. Years later, I still count him as my friend. I have preached at his church, Trinity United Church of Christ, more than once. In fact, one time we packed a Chicago-bound plane with our choir and over 100 people to share in worship and enjoy a special celebration at that historic church.

Within a few months of the campaign, the spit hit the fan alright. My friend was plastered all over the left-leaning so-called "fake news" media (which is often fairer and more balanced than the far-right leaning opinion media). Lead stories and headlines around the country pictured my friend in a fiery sermon shouting, "Damn America!" That friend was (and still is) Dr. Jeremiah Wright, my black brother. He and I are light years apart as it relates to the Bible we both preach, and I have white friends who can't stand him. Yet, he is my friend. My white Christian friends might not have anyone in their friend circles they disagree with theologically, but I don't shy away from opportunities to display another way to mine.

Time after time, I have felt this tension. Too many times I've felt forced to choose between my color and my convictions. But the more I think about it, the more I realize that race and religion have been strange bedfellows as far back as the birth of this nation. Sometimes at odds. More times than not, regrettably, walking in lockstep, and all too often in symbiotic complicity. The religious implications of the philosophy, values, and driving forces behind the birth of this country are seldom highlighted in—even less often connected to—the story and history of racism in this land of the free and home of the brave.

When I was a kid in elementary school, I remember Thanksgiving being a time of stuffed turkey and the stovepipe hats of the Pilgrims. I always thought these were very religious people who fled Britain for religious freedom and the right to serve God according to their beliefs without persecution. I believed they met these nice Indian guys who rode horses with no saddles and had their hair in two ponytails on both sides of the red faces. These guys were nice guys who shared and allowed the Pilgrims to hunt turkeys and build houses on their land. I think that was the first scene in U.S. history that was "photoshopped."

Historian Howard Zinn wrote in his book *A People's History of The United States* that these original inhabitants of this "new world" were "so naïve and so free with their possessions that no one who has not witnessed them would believe it. When you ask for something they have, they never say no. To the contrary, they offer to share with anyone."[106]

Zinn wrote that in return for a little help from his sponsoring

---

106   Zinn, Howard. *A People's History of The United States*. Longman; New York (1980; p.3).

majesties, Christopher Columbus stated he would provide "as much gold...and as many slaves as they ask" and signed off with, "Thus the eternal God, our Lord, gives victory to those who follow His way over apparent impossibilities."[107] I wonder, the "apparent impossibilities" that such guileless and giving people could exist in this world. That "those who follow His way" means Columbus believed God considered getting free gold and slaves from innocent indigenous Americans a "victory." His statement is fraught with moral implications and runneth over with biblical ignorance.

I, like most Americans in the Boomer generation, was taught that Columbus "discovered" America. This is an interesting revelation. How does one "discover" a land that has already been occupied? How do you walk into another man's house, look around, and say, "*Nice discovery. I'll have this*"? While in Haiti, Columbus unashamedly waved the flag of Christianity and reportedly said, "Let us in the name of the Holy Trinity go on sending all the slaves that can be sold."[108] Whatever a man and a nation sow, that shall also be reaped. (Galatians 6:7)

In his amazing article in "Open Theology," South African scholar Bosco B. Bae cites Nico Vorster, noting, "In some respects, the birth of racism in the U.S. begins with religiously justified exploitation, massacre and war with the Native Americans—although an explicit racist ideology in the U.S. did not fully develop until after the abolition of slavery."[109]

As with Africans when they were brought to the slave camps of America, the most effective and dangerous weapon used by the settlers was not the canons or the short wheel-lock carbines, not the blunderbuss prototype of the shotgun or the flintlock pistols or even matchlock muskets.[110] No, the most effective "weapon" they wielded

---

107   Ibid.
108   Ibid., p.4.
109   Bae, Bosco B. "Christianity and Implicit Racism in the U.S. Moral and Human Economy." *Open Theology*, 2016; 2: 1002.
110   "Thanksgiving Leftovers; The Guns of the Pilgrims", Guns.com, 11/25/11. https://www.

against helpless populations kidnapped from their homes thousands of miles away was the *Bible*, the very Word of God. The slave traders and owners "appealed" to the Bible, in Psalm 2:8: "Ask of me, and I shall give thee, the heathen for thine inheritance, and the uttermost parts of the earth for thy possession." And to justify their use of force to take the land, they cited Romans 13:2: "Whatsoever therefore resisteth the power, resisteth the ordinance of God: and they that resist shall receive to themselves damnation."[111] More deadly to the spirit than the cannon, more fatal to the mind than a shot to the head, more destructive than a wildfire, the Word of God was a weapon formed against them—and did it ever prosper.

It is tremendously disheartening when the enemy distorts the power and truth of the Word of God. The prophet Isaiah sought to comfort and encourage the people of God when He declared, "No weapon that is formed against you shall prosper." (Isaiah 54:17; KJV) The Hebrew word for *prosper* means to succeed, to be victorious, to become prosperous. The word assumes the weapon chosen is powerful and that it is intended to be successful. In my humble opinion, I suspect that the prophet never expected that the weapon being used would be the very Word of God. However, the prophecy is turned upside down in the ungodly use of the Word of God as the very weapon of ungodliness. The motive behind the user of the weapon of the Word would in fact succeed in the intended goal of subduing, emasculating, and enslaving its hearers. It is a painful lesson that has been the principle behind charlatans, pulpit pimps, and holy hustlers throughout the history of the church.

In the same like-mindedness of the Pharisees, they used the Word to enslave rather than liberate. The *Dictionary of Biblical Imagery* states, "Though they are considered expert exegetes in the nuance of the law, Jesus condemns them as teachers of the

guns.com/news/2011/11/25/thanksgiving-leftovers-the-guns-of-the-pilgrims
111    Bae, Bosco B. "Christianity and Implicit Racism in the U.S. Moral and Human Economy." *Open Theology*, 2016; 2: 1003.

law for expanding its intention."[112] It is as if the "discoverers" realized how powerful the Word was in converting a soul in the direction of the God of the Word—deciding to use that same power to convert free minds to a slave mentality, paying homage to their owners who introduced that life-changing power to them in the first place—and used it instead with oppressive intentions. I struggle to accept these Pharisaic settlers' supposed "sincerity" in dispensing their understanding of the Word to their own advantage as justification for the strategy. Some may have been sincere, but more like sincerely *wrong*.

The *Dictionary of Biblical Imagery* reports,

> "In the Gospels the words Pharisee and hypocrite are nearly synonymous. The etymology of hypocrite suggests 'a pretender.' In Hebrew culture the Pharisees pretended to be the authoritative opinion on righteousness and the law. They are convincing: fervently loyal to God, zealous for knowledge of Scripture, respected as the authority even by those who disagreed with them. Jesus challenges their right to their assumed position and exposes their pretense and emerges as a higher authority. The Pharisees defend their stance aggressively, ultimately collaborating in Jesus' death."[113]

The settlers' pseudo-Pharisaic image would ultimately lead to the virtual near extinction of the native Americans who "welcomed" them, and to the establishment of the institution of slavery. It would be just like God to providentially use the same Book that was used to enslave humanity, to be the root of the tree of liberation of the very victims of those who "meant it for evil." God

---

112  *Dictionary of Biblical Imagery* © 1998 by InterVarsity Christian Fellowship/USA.
113  Ibid.

would turn it around for Kingdom good. In a real sense, any black man who believes the Bible, is a miracle.

It is allowable to acknowledge (though not to approve) the dastardly behavior of those who came to these shores as historical "Soldiers of the cross...coming to hold up the blood stained banner" (of the Lord).[114] In this new land, one might say their actions were birthed out of their sincere love for the God whose Word they would misuse. One might give them the benefit of the doubt. However, I suspect there is unintended evidence of the contents of their hearts. From James Walvin in *All You Need to Know*:

> "Slave owners have little trouble reconciling daily brutality with their Christian faith. William Byrd, a prosperous Virginian tobacco planer, wrote in his diary in 1709: I took a walk about the plantation. Eugene was whipped for running away and had the [bit] put on him. I said my prayers and had good health and good thoughts, and good humor, thanks be to God Almighty."[115]

How happily and cavalierly they went about their dark business of oppressing the brutally kidnapped and enslaved.

When the hands of time began to tick-tock toward the demise of "legal" slavery and the opposition of abolitionism began to rise up, "part of the opposition to Abolitionism derived from the continued conviction that slavery was compatible with Christianity," writes Jeremy Black in *Slavery; A New Global History*. He continues, "...that it was sanctioned by its existence in the Bible, notably the Old Testament, an argument that indicates the range of views that could be squeezed from Christian teaching, and the Christian heritage."[116]

---

114  © 2011 Hymnlyrics.org & Carden's Design. This website is privately owned and operated. Webmaster Kevin Carden.

115  Walvin, James. *All You Need to Know...Slavery: The History and Legacy of One of The World's Most Brutal Institutions*. Malta; Connell Publishing (2018; p. 860).

116  Black, Jeremy. *Slavery; A New Global History*. Running Press, Philadelphia (p. 160).

I find it interesting and somewhat ironic that this same observation of Christian hypocrisy was noted and voiced by one of our past U.S. Presidents, who might be considered by some to be a right-wing conservative proponent and product of the mindset of generations of southern slave holders.

On his 2003 visit to Africa, George W. Bush, 43rd President of the United States, traveled to the West African slave-trading post at Gorée, Senegal. Bush, a conservative, right-wing Republican, is quoted by Jeremy Black:

> "Christian men and women became blind to the clearest commands of their faith....Enslaved Africans discovered a suffering Savior and found him as more like themselves than their masters. This same point had been made by the Abolitionist Stephen Cave, who wrote that 'the African owes his degradation to his intercourse with the inhabitants of enlightened Christian Europe.'"[117]

Even some of the blacks who regarded Bush among their political enemies, would at least give him credit for being right that one time.

Again, back to the chilly D.C., Mall on Inauguration Day. I stood with thousands there on the cusp of history. I was close enough to see the stage, but I could more clearly see the long staircase where this majestic black man and his beautiful Nubian wife would take the walk down the stairs and up into the history books. It was a long way from the shores of the Pilgrim settlers and the tobacco and cotton fields of black slaves who would never have dreamed of this day. They dreamed of a land where "trouble don't last always." They dreamed that "soon (they) would be done

---

[117]   Ibid.

wid de troubles of dis world." They never dreamed that one day a black man would live in the White House that slaves built, a black man who had no slaves on his paternal side (as President Obama's father was a black man born in Kenya, Africa) or on his maternal side (as his mother was a Caucasian woman born in Kansas, America). He was a pure representation of the ideal: a child born of a non-slave union of black and white.

I don't know if my white brothers and sisters can imagine—or if they even care—how historically significant it was for a black man to occupy the White House. When the President's house began in 1792, there was an effort to import workers from Europe to meet the labor needs for construction. This effort produced two levels of success: little and none. In light of the dearth of white European workers, the commissioners of Washington D.C., turned to African Americans, both slaves and free blacks. The slaves were trained on the spot at the government's quarry at Aquia, Virginia, as quarrymen, sawyers, brick-makers and carpenters. "The wage rolls for May 1795 list enslaved persons Tom, Peter, Ben, Harry and Daniel, four of whom were owned by White House architect James Hoban. Daniel was owned by Hoban's assistant, Pierce Purcell," states a press fact sheet on the history of the White House, adding that slave labor, as well as free labor, was also used during the 1814-1818 rebuilding of the White House following the War of 1812. [118]

It goes without saying that U.S. Presidents who occupied the White House brought their slaves into the President's house upon election. Slave owner, President Andrew Jackson, brought a large household of enslaved people with him from Tennessee to the President's house. These slaves were put under the direction of Antoine Michel Guista, the steward of the White House. Many white servants were thus replaced by the less expensive labor of enslaved workers. The U.S. government itself did not own slaves, but

---

118   White House History. https://www.whitehousehistory.org/press-room/press-fact-sheets/slavery-and-the-white-house

hired them from their masters.[119]

The mother of President Theodore Roosevelt (who officially named the executive mansion the "White House" in 1901) was from a Southern plantation family that owned slaves. According to a PBS television program called "Slavery by Another Name...,"

> "Roosevelt's attitudes on race fluctuated, though he was generally considered a moderate during his era. He ended school segregation in New York. He invited black civil rights activist, Booker T. Washington, to dine at the White House. The backlash from his supporters rose up against him. He never repeated the gesture. His support began to shrink, and he backed off of his more aggressive efforts and became more passive in his support."[120]

It's interesting that Roosevelt is painted as a Progressive with sensitivities toward black people. A classic example is the invitation he gave to black activist Booker T. Washington. However, in accordance with the "hermeneutic of suspicion" (which basically assumes there is more to a given story than meets the eye), if you look a little deeper and ask a few more questions, you find that the picture of this moderately progressive presidential leader might not be as close to the moderate center as some have portrayed him. Indeed, Roosevelt actually challenged Jim Crow laws but was not an advocate of civil rights and held that blacks were intellectually inferior.

We learn from Tsahai Tafari in the PBS program "The Rise and Fall of Jim Crow...,"

---

119   Ibid. Don't fall into the trap of legitimizing slavery in this picture by thinking that at least they were being paid: a "paid slave" is an oxymoron, tantamount to the so-called "pay" that slaves received for share cropping.
120   "Slavery by Another Name"; PBS.org.

"The executive administrations of 1876-1900 did not address legislation designed to disfranchise Blacks, such as poll taxes, grandfather clauses, intimidation, and lynching. The election of Theodore Roosevelt in 1904 heralded one of the first Presidential administrations openly opposed to civil rights and suffrage for Blacks. Roosevelt is remembered for inviting the Black leader and entrepreneur, Booker T. Washington, to the White House for dinner, the first instance of such an invitation for a Black person. Southern Democrats were offended and were vocal in their disapproval. Though Washington's visit was distinctive in its novelty, Roosevelt invited Washington not to improve the situation of Blacks, but because they agreed that Blacks should not strive for political and social equality. Washington privately used his wealth and influence to challenge Jim Crow, despite his public declarations of the opposite, while Roosevelt's administration was not supportive of civil rights for Blacks. The popularity of eugenics and the philosophy of social Darwinism reached a zenith during the early part of century, and racism was integrated into presidential party platforms as late as the early 1930s. President Roosevelt believed Blacks were intellectually inferior, and began to decrease the number of federal appointments to Blacks and promised Southerners that he would appoint local federal officials that would not disrupt the accord between north and south."[121]

In her book, *Theodore Roosevelt and American Racism*, Margaret Kimberley adds even more surprising revelations about America's two-term 26th President, whose face adorns Mount Rushmore, served as the nation's 25th Vice President, was a former

---

121   Tafari, Tsahai; "The Rise and Fall of Jim Crow." PBS.org (see: https://www.thirteen.org/wnet/jimcrow/print/p_struggle_president.html )

Governor of New York and leader of the Republican Party, stating that "Roosevelt also urged White people to make babies in order to conquer the colored masses of the world. In a lengthy discourse that has come to be known as the 'race suicide letter' he stated that anyone who didn't reproduce was 'in effect a criminal against the race.'"[122]

Once again to the Mall on that chilly Tuesday, January 20, 2009. I looked around and saw black men carrying their sons and daughters on their shoulders. I saw several people fighting to swab their leaky eyes, as was I. *Black man in the White House.* Wow.

I am 71 years old at this writing in 2019. The nation is gearing up for another election. Two black people are running; a black woman and another black man. A highly regarded black legislator, Congressman Elijah Cummings, acknowledged leader and champion for the rights of the oppressed everywhere, passed away in mid-October. As my mind pushes the rewind button and I recall that historic chilly day, watching the Obamas step into U.S.—and world—history, I wonder if there will be a repeat performance for America. Or at least a rerun in my lifetime.

Could there be *two black faces* hanging in the Hall of Presidents in the White House in my lifetime? How many people, I wonder, are huddled in secret rooms saying, "They had their time. It's time for a Latino"? "They had their shot. It is time for a woman"? "Time for a black woman"? Is this election about race, all over again? Is it about the twin-civil rights hot topic, *time for a black woman!* And what of the huddle of middle and upper-class white men who are determined not to let the White House slip from their fingers? Or their black counterparts determined to *take this thing back*? Where is the room that has symbolically voted already and concluded that it's time to take this country back from the right- or

---

122   Kimberley, Margaret; Theodore Roosevelt and American Racism. Global Research. September 18, 2014. https://www.globalrearch.ca/theodore-roosevelt-and-american-racism/5402633.

left-leaning philosophy of *that other party*? The *other*, who've decided it's time to make America *anything else* again.

It seems not to matter so much about political ideas as it does what color the face is that oversees the most powerful nation in the world—grasping at its last straws of such power, as it increasingly appears lately (After all, *every* great empire in history fades away.).

As always, and once again...the walls of division are firmly in place.

Can these walls fall? Will we allow them to fall—*insist* that, for the glory of God, they fall?

Stay tuned.

# 9
# YOU DON'T LOOK LIKE YOUR PICTURE

*"When I look out at this convention, I see the face*
*of America, red, yellow, brown, black and white.*
*We are all precious in God's sight...."*
—**Jesse Jackson**[123]


*I remember my Uncle Jess and Aunt Indie (short for Indiana)*
*packing a lunch of fried chicken, a loaf of white bread (Wonder Bread!)*
*and some pound cake into a shoe box and boarding a bus to travel for*
*days to Washington D.C., for the March on Washington, led by Dr.*
*Martin Luther King, Jr.*

*I remember boycotts against the Walgreens store on Collinsville*
*Avenue, the main commercial drag in E. St. Louis.*

*I remember being turned away from the Admiral when I was a*
*child.*

*I remember the lady at the ritzy hotel in Dallas tossing me her*
*keys to park her SUV.*

*I remember so many countless other incidents of overt racism*
*against me and others of my skin color over my decades on God's earth*
*that one book could not contain them all (though my memoir might*
*one day come close).*

*Yet, the closest I've ever come to personal involvement in*
*joining in "the struggle" was when I was forced into it by accident*
*that day at the university. Did that count? Did being an accidental*
*revolutionary based strictly on the color of my skin make me a soldier*
*in the war against racism? Even a tiny bit? Or am I doing my share*

---

123   Speech at the Democratic National Convention, Atlanta, Georgia; July 19, 1988.

*by simply being a black man making his way through one of the most wonderful, most beautiful, most powerful, most racist nations on earth...*

\* \* \*

One of the many areas the Lord is still working on in my life is patience. I'm getting better. I am not as impatient as I used to be. But I still struggle with it. I want patience (And I want it *now!*).

I learned a great lesson in patience several years ago. I was invited to preach somewhere in the Midwest. I was told I would be picked up when I landed by a man from the host church. I really do not like to wait around. I made my way off the plane to the baggage area and looked for the sign with my name, which was often there to welcome me. No sign. No name. I do not like to wait.

I treaded through the hustling, bustling crowd of people getting their luggage and saw no one who looked like he was looking for someone. When there were only a few people left in the baggage area, rather than wait, I gathered my bags and began to impatiently pace around, wondering where the guy was who was supposed to pick me up.

Soon, the luggage from another flight came down the conveyor, and the area filled with the next group of travelers in search of their belongings. No sign of the guy. I hate waiting. Finally, after what seemed like an eternity of 40 or 45 minutes, I was nearly all alone again in the baggage area, walking back and forth. It was just me and one lone elderly gentleman sitting on a bench and airport workers going about their work.

I slowed down as the man on the bench seemed to be trying to make eye contact with me. After straining to see my face, he asked, "Hey, are you Reverend Ulmer?"

I stopped in front of him and said, "Yes, sir. That's me."

He began to laugh while frantically pulling a photo from the inside pocket of his jacket. He looked at the picture. He looked at me. He looked at the picture.

He said, "Awww, Reverend! I been looking for you for over an hour! Aww, Reverend, I'm sorry. But Reverend, you don't look like your picture."

He had passed right by me several times, for over an hour, but because I didn't look like my picture, he never said a word. And I had been expecting a guy holding up a sign.

In the midst of the division, fractures, and factions in our society, I wonder how many times people pass right by because we don't look like their picture of us.

The family of Christian denominations seldom reflects the unity for which Jesus prayed. In their excellent work, challenging the Southern Baptist Convention, titled *Removing the Stain of Racism from the Southern Baptist Convention*, speaking as constituents of the reputed second largest religious organization in America (second only to Catholicism), Jarvis Williams and Kevin Jones, Sr., wrote:

> "Throughout history, racial ideologies have been driving forces of war, of social cohesion, of demagoguery, and of dictatorships. Race theory was central to the Nazi regime and was used by both sides in the Pacific theater of World War II. In that theater of the war, both the Japanese and the Americans claimed the other was an inferior race that must be defeated by force. The Japanese claimed racial superiority as central to their subjugation of other Asian peoples."[124]

White superiority was the mindset of many Americans in the World War II era. "The main 'color line,' as Frederick Douglass

---

124  Williams, Jarvis. J., Jones, Kevin M. Sr., *Removing the Stain of Racism from the Southern Baptist Convention*. Nashville: B&H Academic. 2017. Kendle Edition. Location 756 of 3574.

called it in 1881, has always been black and white in America."[125] Williams and Jones wrote, "White superiority was claimed as a belief by both Abraham Lincoln and Jefferson Davis, but the Confederacy made racial superiority a central purpose. More humbling still is the fact that many churches, churchmen, and theologians gave sanction to that ideology of racial superiority."[126]

Founded in 1845, Southern Baptists were certainly not the only proponents of this racial arrogance. Slavery was the soil from which denominational distinctions brought forth a harvest that was indicative of the broader society and would become a point of contention leading to organizational splits in the Presbyterian family, as well.

Denominational distinctives would meet at the ideology of racial superiority and a theology that affirmed a saying that was the common ground between those who argued over polity in my neighborhood: *If it's white, it's right, and if it's black, get back.* It was a horrendous belief held by racist ecclesiastical "scholars."

I had an academic experience in several of my first classes in seminary, where every now and then I would hear phrases like, "Josephus says..." Or, "We learn this from Josephus." Or, "Josephus gives us additional insight into...." I thought maybe I had missed this Josephus, until I learned he was not a biblical character. In his article "Is Josephus Reliable?—Biblical History" in *Answers* magazine, Brenton H. Cook explains:

> "Famed Jewish historian Josephus Flavius was born in Jerusalem in AD 37 or 38, not long after Christ's crucifixion. The son of a priest, he became a Pharisee, a military commander in the Jewish resistance, and an eyewitness to Jerusalem's destruction in AD 70. Eusebius, the first church historian, calls him 'the most famous Jew

---

125  Ibid.
126  Ibid.

of his time' and tells of a statue erected in his honor in Rome."[127]

There is disagreement on whether or not Josephus actually became a Christian. One online information website states, "Not being a Christian himself (in his day the Christians comprised a mystical branch of Judaism) it would have been unlikely that Josephus would have even considered the actual Jesus as divine."[128]

However, I suggest Josephus's soul condition is less important than the credibility he has been given as a research resource for students of the Bible by certain intellectual gatekeepers. It's important to understand that Josephus was a first century secular Jewish historian and an observer of the culture and times of the early New Testament, particularly the times of Jesus and the first church. The *Dictionary of New Testament Background* gives further background on Josephus:

> "The writings of Flavius Josephus ( A.D. 37-c. 100) constitute by far the most important body of literature for the background of Christianity. It is Josephus who tells us almost everything we know about the non-Christian figures, groups, institutions, customs, geographical areas and events mentioned in the NT. He is the only surviving contemporary writer, for example, who describes John the Baptist, the Jewish high priests of the first century, the Pharisees and Sadducees, the various regions of Judea, Samaria and Galilee, Herod the Great, Agrippa II and Berenice, the Jerusalem temple renovated by Herod and its destruction in the revolt of 66-74, the census under Quirinius, Judas the Galilean, Theudas and the Egyptian prophet."[129]

---

127   Cook, Brenton H. "Is Josephus Reliable?—Biblical History" *Answers Magazine*. January 1, 2013. https://answersingenesis.org/bible-history/is-josephus-reliable/
128   Rational Josephus; Wiki. See: https://rationalwiki.org/wiki/Josephus
129   *Dictionary of New Testament Background*, edited by Craig A. Evans and Stanley E.

As I sat in class after class, I learned the value of objective contributors who produced works outside of the books of Bible and filled in significant historical, contextual gaps in the biblical story of the early books of the New Testament. My style of preaching leans heavily on the attempt to transport the listener to the setting of the text, passage, or narrative that capture our attention for the message. Information and revelation that came from Josephus aids in activating our sanctified imagination and time travels us to the dusty roads of the land of the Gospels and the life and times of Jesus and the disciples. I learned the value of the writings of Josephus as a hermeneutic and homiletic tool from the very beginning of my ministry journey, which has captured my life for over 40 years. The *Dictionary of New Testament Background* continues:

> "...Scholars are coming to realize that Josephus writes about these matters because he has stories to tell. And those stories represent the most fully articulated statements of first-century Judaism in Judea that we possess. They are told by a contemporary of the first and second Christian generations who came from circles very different from Jesus' followers: from a member of the governing aristocratic priesthood. Josephus's narratives are important, then, both because they represent a different view of the same conditions that the NT mentions and because they provide the indispensable context for understanding what Josephus says about Herod, Pilate, the temple, and so on."[130]

Here's where we are so far in this exegesis of Josephus: Biblical scholars accept, use, and legitimize the value and use of extra-biblical resources that add nuance, fill in blanks, and provoke

---

Porter, © 2000 by InterVarsity Christian Fellowship/USA. Published by InterVarsity Press. InterVarsity Press, Downers Grove, IL.
130  Ibid.

deeper and expanded contemplation on the story of Scripture. Josephus Flavius was an example of just such valued resources. He held some of the missing pieces in the puzzle of the picture of the people of God in the museum of the Bible story. On a more practical level, the historical hermeneutical value of such utilizing an extra-canonic resource sets the stage for the legitimate continuation of such a practice when zooming in the exegetical lens on textual gaps and the questions which arise from such an investigation into the complexity of the topic of racism.

I think the first time I ventured down the path that would lead to Josephus-like questions was in an Old Testament class. I'm not sure if was an OT Survey class or maybe one on the Pentateuch, the first five books of the Bible. Nevertheless, as I recall, we were studying Noah and the flood. When the obvious question of how the post-flood world would be populated arose, the discussion lead to the different races. And here is where I got confused—very confused.

OK, so here I am sitting in a class, taking notes, and I suddenly realize what I'm writing. So, according to the storyline, here is this assumed white Noah who has three kids: one white, one black, one kind of yellow-brownish. I'm thinking: *You gotta be kidding me.* Because, by now I have a couple of problems. First of all, I can't get ready for this explanation that the white Noah had a black baby. Second, my mind does a black-history flashback: I grew up being told that it only takes one drop of black blood to make you black. (Maybe the law was one-sixteenth or one-thirty-second, whatever the "pre-historic" edict was in America regarding when people got to call us black, or worse.)

Nevertheless, the one-drop rule was a social and legal principle of racial classification grounded in the anthropological concept of hypodescent, which is the automatic assignment of children of a mixed union between socioeconomic or ethnic groups to the group with the lower status. This means that if we all descended from a black woman in Africa, which recent DNA studies indicate, we're all black. Period. End of story.

Here's how F. James Davis's *Who is Black? One Nation's Definition* defined it in a PBS's "Frontline" television program:

> "The nation's answer to the question 'Who is black?' has long been that a black is any person with **any** known African black ancestry. This definition reflects the long experience with slavery and later with Jim Crow segregation. In the South, it became known as the 'one-drop rule,' meaning that a single drop of 'black blood' makes a person a black. It is also known as the 'one black ancestor rule,' some courts have called it the 'traceable amount rule,' and anthropologists call it the 'hypo-descent rule,' meaning that racially mixed persons are assigned the status of the subordinate group. This definition emerged from the American South to become the nation's definition, generally accepted by whites and blacks. Blacks had no other choice."[131]

I was offended. Offended that this was the "explanation" white people were giving out. It was their story, and they were sticking to it. I'm like, "You don't really expect me to believe this, do you?" Well, shame on you. The lingering question marks in my mind on the race issue have loomed over me and my teaching/preaching ministry for decades. I have tactfully, and sometimes not so tactfully, danced around, side-stepped, and learned to fake it 'till I could make it, in discussions, classes, and messages that directly or indirectly touched on the race issue. The explanations just didn't make sense. I have seen the pendulum swing wide from one extreme to the polar opposite. Most of the books in my library related to

---

131   Davis, F. James. "Who is Black? One Nation's Definition"; "Frontline," PBS SoCal website, WGBH educational foundation.

the reality of the different races and colors in the world likewise sidestepped or faked the ultimate question of where we came from, leaving the assumption on the table that the God-story, the biblical account, is filled with white people only.

On the other extreme, I have several books that take the position that the Bible is filled with black people. In fact, some extremist positions suggest that everybody in the Bible was black, and there were no white people in the Bible at all. What's a guy going to do? So, where do you land on this issue? What is a legitimate and what is a ludicrous oversimplification that paints everyone with a one-color broad brush where there is little or no diversity at all? And then I remembered old man Joe! Josephus popped into my mind. In fact, I discovered a Josephus-type, extra-biblical resource.

Let me quickly say that I claim no trail-blazer status. I don't claim to be the discoverer of a long-hidden resource. In fact, I have found myself frustrated and resentful that the resource has been around so very long, but I suspect it has been suppressed by the intellectual ecclesiastical gatekeepers because it not only does not line up with the more popular, traditional explanations of the conservative academy and pulpit, but it challenges the character and content of the voices of the white religious establishment.

Now let's go to the deep end of the pool.

# 10
# GOD IS ON OUR SIDE

*"Winners and losers*
*Fight when you know you're right*
*You'll get some bruises but*
*Some fool might see the light."*
—**Main Ingredient**[132]

*Nowadays, I wonder: Did I sleep through the revolution? Looking back on it, I realize I was almost in a matrix zone of disconnection.*

*Other than that one night, my campus had been relatively quiet during the revolution. Indeed, the Watts Riots, Chicago, Detroit, D.C.,—all of the uprisings across America made few, if any, significant ripples on the mid-America home of the Fighting Illini. There were no campus-wide, organized marches, sit-ins, or protests by the few black students on the campus during those tumultuous times. I wonder if we were waiting for it to be televised, thrust in our faces, forcing us kids to make a deliberate decision to join in or sit out.*

*Could I have done more over the ensuing years? Should I have? Or have I been edging ever closer to it by writing this book? Because there's something happening here in America. And what it is, is exactly clear. The walls of division are undergoing a stress test like never before. Walls can fall...but only if we insist.*

\* \* \*

As I mentioned earlier, you have never been in a fight until you take the battlefield against someone who believes God is

---

132   "Think"; by Ted White & Aretha Franklin, on the album "Aretha Now." See: https://genius.com/Aretha-franklin-think-lyrics

on his or her side. The fundamental driving force behind the seemingly unending war in the Middle East is that both sides feel they are on a mission from God. In the 1980 movie, *The Blues Brothers*, Jake and Elwood, reunite after a stint in prison. They have an unusual attachment to the nuns and school they attended as boys. Driven by the passionate commitment to raise money to improve the orphanage, they humbly justify any lawbreaking actions with the battle cry, "We're on a mission from God." They fearlessly set out to "raise" the money assured that their mission would be accomplished because it was divinely ordained. They go back into show business by putting their old band together and creatively calling it "The Blues Brother Band." One of the scenes pictures the late, great Aretha Franklin warning her musician husband who is about to go on the road with the band, "You better think; think about what 'cha trying to do to me."[133] Jake and Elwood confidentially maneuver against the law and lawmen with the backing of the God who works in mysterious ways. God is on their side.

This mysterious mandate by the Master is actually the essence of the ideology and theology that established a nation. It is the unrighteous religion of the founding fathers, grounded in the interpretation—or I should say misinterpretation—of the Curse on Ham, that justified slavery. They believed they were on a mission from God. They truly and sincerely believed God was on their side. They were sincere. They were sincerely wrong.

This hermeneutical blunder birthed racism in this country. I want to take a closer look at their position, and I want to look at it utilizing the acceptable interpretive method of extra-biblical resources that fill in the blanks and give complimentary perspectives allowing a broader more comprehensive view of the texts in question. I want to zoom the lens in and out and take note of the

---

133   Ibid.

shades and shadows of the light we shine on the texts and the light that comes forth from the texts.

We have noted that slavery, and the racist mindset that imported and expanded it, was not just a jaded colonization philosophy of the descendants of the Mayflower. It was the mentality of the fledgling nation. "Everybody's doing it," would be a fair conclusion of even the most casual historian's research.

It's indicative of what was happening in the culture. A whole culture for generations thought slavery was okay. More than okay—that it was *right*. More than right—that it was *godly!* Slavery? Godly? Show me chapter and verse where God, and not man, ordained slavery and the subjection of one's fellow man under a good and right and godly enterprise. It's not in the Bible.

From some of my well-meaning white friends, I sometimes hear questions like: "Why don't y'all just get over that slavery thing? Why don't you get past it and just forget about it? It's over and done with."

I like how my Jewish friends respond to that attitude. Not only do they vow to never forget the Holocaust, they vow "Never again!" They will never forget the killing of over 6 million Jews, and they won't let the world forget either. That may be a lesson for us to learn. They say *Never again!* We too have to take a stance that racial iniquities can never happen again. Injustice and crime and criminality and death and lack of justice in the justice system—*Never again! Not on my watch!* Somebody has to take a stand and say, "No more!" It can start with one voice. One shout. One determined mind. It can start in your piece of the world, your neighborhood, your home.

Marginalized cultures and peoples don't just traipse intentionally to the outskirts of society on their own or be happily relegated to the margins. They are thrust to the margins, forced to the edges, given no other choice. But once they find themselves on the other side of the tracks, they soon realize that where they are has been systematically structured to keep them in that place. It is a strategy of deception of satanic proportions.

The racist American mind is traced back to the pillars of an ideology and a theology. We have seen that the source of the theology of racism hangs on the so-called Curse of Ham that is used as validation of the hierarchy of races, especially the hierarchy that places whites at the top and black and other people of color below. So, we might find insight that helps us unravel this historical theology as we take another deeper look at this family of Noah and the so-called curse that placed succeeding generations of people of color at the bottom.

Heads up: I'm going to repeat some ideas we have discussed before. I want to put some of these ideas in the context of going deeper down and further into the concept of color, race and racism as the basis of slavery.

However, for the purpose of this brief encore, it is important to know that this so-called curse *is the theological basis of American racism*. Moreover, the theory was birthed, nursed, matured, and cherished by advocates of a theology that was supposedly the roots of European settlers seeking religious freedom in America. Indeed, Christian denominations were founded by men who held to an ideology of racial superiority and bathed that ideology in the scandalous theological argument involving a curse Noah put on Ham's son Canaan. At times, white superiority was defended by the claim that this "Curse of Ham" was the explanation for dark skin—an outrageous, biblically unsupported, and wholly unsound argument that reflects such ignorance of Scripture and such shameful exegesis that it could only be believed by those who were *deliberately looking* for an argument to satisfy their prejudices.[134]

Denominational founders historically neglected (and many still neglect) to teach about people of color, including Africans/

---

134   Williams, Jarvis. J., Jones, Kevin M. Sr., *Removing the Stain of Racism from the Southern Baptist Convention*. Nashville: B&H Academic. 2017. Kindle Edition. Location 773 of 3574.

blacks, who played significant roles in the Old and New Testaments. I suggest that most, even today, view biblical characters as being white, including, and maybe especially, Jesus.

"The belief that all biblical characters are white can lead to a conscious or subconscious conclusion that whites are superior to people of color," write Williams and Jones.[135] Kudos to such bold soldiers as Dr. R. Albert Mohler, Jr., who, speaking at a chapel service at Southern Baptist Theological Seminary in 2015 addressing "The Table of the Nations, the Tower of Babel, and the Marriage Supper of the Lamb: Ethnic Diversity and the Radical Vision of the Gospel of Jesus Christ," declared, "African and Asiatic people may well be rooted in the sons of Ham." Williams and Jones accurately note: "The implications of his statement are staggering. It places Hamitic peoples/Africans in the bloodline of Jesus and underscores their prominence in the Old Testament."[136]

As we studied earlier, Genesis 9:20-17 is the unfortunate passage used as the foundation of the misinterpretation. After the flood, after the docking of the ark on dry land, God blessed Noah and his family. God established what would come to be called the Noahic Covenant. In it, God promised He would never again destroy the earth with a flood. (Genesis 9:8-17) Later, Noah got drunk and naked, and his son Ham, father of Canaan, saw him. Noah's sons Shem and Japheth took a garment and walked backward toward their father and covered him—not looking upon his nakedness. Noah awakens...and curses *Canaan*. Whoa! So that's the first problem. Ham was not cursed. His son Canaan was cursed to be a servant to his brothers. So, technically, Noah cursed his grandson. What's up with that?

Scholars have come up with all kinds of interpretations of this passage:

135   Ibid. Location 2733 of 3574.
136   Ibid. Location 2742 of 3574.

"Many interpreters believe Ham's sin was voyeurism or a homosexual advance on his father, Noah. In the 19th century, it was not uncommon for Bible teachers and preachers to assume Ham was cursed along with Canaan and that black skin was the curse. Such logic is convoluted to say the least.... Ham was the biblical progenitor of 'Cush, Egypt, Put' (Gen 10:6). **Cush** is regarded by biblical scholars as Ethiopia, while **Put** is apparently either Libya or Somalia. Together with **Egypt**, these three nations descended from Ham (the 'Hamitic' peoples) are densely populated with native people with dark or black skin. This led to the flawed conclusion that—despite the fact it was Canaan, not Ham, who was cursed—God must have turned the skin of Ham and his descendants black in response to Noah's cursing."[137]

So, they were wrong. Very wrong. Yet it became fodder for the flame of racism contaminating the soil of the seeds of "democracy."

Let's take another look. What about color? Noah, Ham, Canaan—these guys looked like "something." They had skin. It had to look like something. It had to be some color, some hue, some shade. As I have confessed, I grew up thinking everyone in the Bible was white. I was 30 years old before I was corrected. But let's get real. They had to have looked like something; they had skin, and that skin had to have a color to it.

We have established the validity of extra-biblical resources in assisting the hermeneutic of biblical revelation. I offer a resource that sheds light on this period: The Book of Enoch. Now, some discredit this source, because it has been widely used by Mormon scholars, which is interesting. Remember, Josephus was a Jew. According to *Black History in the Bible*, "While the Book of Enoch is not considered

---

137  Heiser, M. S. (2019). "I Dare You Not to Bore Me with the Bible: When Appearances Aren't Misleading." *Bible Study Magazine*, 11(4), 8.

canon (official Scripture), it was very important to the ancient Hebrews. In fact, it was so important, that they hid it among the Dead Sea scrolls at Qumran."[138]

There is debate as to the identity of the writer of the Book of Enoch. Some say Enoch is the generic name for a seer. Others say it was a later prophet by that name. A good number of scholars identify the writer as the name mentioned by the New Testament writer Jude, which puts him in the line of Noah and Adam. This is seen by many as a reference to a passage in the Book of Enoch 1:9, which is unprovable as a quote or tradition. There is question as to whether the author was in the line of Cain (Genesis 5:17) or in the line of Seth (Genesis 5:18-24). "Enoch, the seventh from Adam, prophesied about them: 'See, the Lord is coming with thousands upon thousands of his holy ones.'" (Jude 1:14) "Barnes Notes" says:

> "There is, indeed, now an apocryphal writing called 'the Book of Enoch,' containing a prediction strongly resembling this, but there is no certain proof that it existed so early as the time of Jude, nor, if it did, is it absolutely certain that he quoted from it. Both Jude and the author of that book ['the Book of Enoch'] may have quoted a common tradition of their time, for there can be no doubt that the passage referred to was handed down by tradition. The passage as found in 'the Book of Enoch' is in these words: "Behold he comes with ten thousand of his saints, to execute judgment upon them, and destroy the wicked, and reprove all the carnal, for everything which the sinful and ungodly have done and committed against him," chapter ii. Bib. Repository, vol. xv. p. 86. If the Book of Enoch was written after the time of Jude, it is natural to suppose that the prophecy referred to by him, and

---

138  "The Book of Enoch: Black Adam, Albino Noah, and The Image of God"; *Black History in the Bible*. December 21, 2016. See: http://www.blackhistoryinthebible.com/hidden-history/the-book-of-enoch-black-adam-albino-noah-and-the-color-of-god/

handed down by tradition, would be inserted in it. This book was discovered in an Aethiopic version and was published with a translation by Dr. Laurence of Oxford, in 1821, and republished in 1832."[139]

There is debate about the author of the Book of Enoch, though it is widely acknowledged as a non-divinely inspired resource (as was Josephus). So, let's look at the extra-biblical commentary. Most relevant to our discussion is this passage from the Book of Enoch: "Was everyone on the planet black before Noah's flood? The Book of Enoch seems to indicate that the world before Noah's flood was a much darker place, as far as melanin is concerned. While the Book of Enoch is not considered canon (official Scripture), it was very important to the ancient Hebrews. In fact, it was so important, that they hid it among the Dead Sea scrolls at Qumran."[140] Let's look again at the story concerning Noah's birth:

"After a time, my son Methuselah took a wife for his son Lamech. She became pregnant by him, and brought forth a child, **the flesh of which was as white as snow**, and red as a rose; the hair of whose head was white like wool, and long; and whose eyes were beautiful. When he opened them, he illuminated all the house, like the sun; the whole house abounded with light. And when he was taken from the hand of the midwife, opening also his mouth, he spoke to the Lord of righteousness. Then Lamech his father was afraid of him; and flying away came to his own father Methuselah, and said, I have begotten a son, **unlike to other children**. He is not human but, **resembling the offspring of the angels of heaven**, is of a different nature from ours, being altogether unlike to us."

139   "Barnes' Notes," Electronic Database ©1997-2014, Biblesoft, Inc.
140   *Black History In the Bible*. Ibid.

—Book of Enoch 105:1-3 (bold highlight added).
Several relations come forth from this text:
    1. Noah was born with white skin.
    2. Noah did not look like the other humans.
    3. Lamech believed Noah was the son of an angel.
    4. Angels were having children on earth.

At least two provocative implications emerge:
    1. White skin was not common among humans.
    2. The children of the angels (Nephilim[141]) were white.[142]

Noah's skin was white. His father, Lamech, was afraid of him. I don't take this literally as some do, but I think it is hyperbole indicating how unheard of this white-skinned baby was. The baby had long, wooly hair and beautiful eyes that poetically lit up the room. Lamech is so astonished that he runs to his father, old man Methuselah, and tells the story of the white-skinned baby, Noah, who Lamech said was an oddity. He likens him to angels (whatever he might have thought they looked like), again hyperbolic of this unheard-of scene.

The only logical reason the white-skinned boy was an oddity is because everyone else up to that point in creation history were "colored." Lamech's words, "...being altogether unlike to us," prove that everything about Noah was different, including his skin color."[143]

But wait a minute. How could this colored man have a white baby? Flash back to seminary class. I remember vividly the lesson and the bewilderment in the class where the prof was teaching on creation, and when he got to the after-flood, he suggested that Noah had a white baby, a black baby, and a yellowish baby.

---

141   See: http://ministerfortson.com/category/nehilim-giants
142   *Black History In the Bible.* Ibid.
143   Ibid.

"**The sons of Noah, Shem, Ham, and Japheth**. Most scholars point to Shem, Ham, and Japheth as the progenitors of all the races of earth (Gen. 10). Shem is said to be the father of the Semite races (Jews, Arabs, etc.), Ham the father of the dark-skinned (blacks), and Japheth the father of the Caucasian races (whites). Such a position is based, in part, on the names of some of their descendants and where they later located. For instance, Ham was the father of "Cush" (Gen. 10: 6). The "land of Cush" is later called 'Ethiopia' (Numbers 12: 1)."[144]

And even if that was so, Noah would have had to have at least one drop of black blood in order to make one of his sons black. It made no sense, and I was bewildered that this was the company line. But when you really think about it, it does raise another possibility. "In fact, it is a scientific fact that black people can have white children, but white people cannot have a black child.[145] The only way for all of the races to exist on the planet, is if they started dark, and then became lighter over time."[146]

This means white people cannot have a black baby, but black people can have a white baby! A black baby with white skin is called an albino. White Lamech had a baby of a frightening color—white—because everyone before Noah had colored skin. Enoch, Lamech, and Noah were all from the line of Seth (Adam's third son). If they were people of color, it also indicates that Seth was a man of color, which would also make Adam a man of color.

The story of Adam takes you back to Genesis 2:7, where we learn that Adam was created from the dust of the earth. Actually, by

---

144  "The Origin of the Races"; *Bible Truths.* See: http://www.bibletruths.net/archives/BTAROO6.htm

145  See: http://www.blackhistoryinthebible.com/the-gentiles/unmasking-the-gentiles-the-greatest-deception-on-earth-part-1

146  *Black History in the Bible.* Barnes' Notes, Electronic Database ©1997-2014, Biblesoft, Inc. See: http://www.blackhistoryinthebible.com/hidden-history/the-book-of-enoch-black-adam-albino-noah-and-the-color-of-god/

the time God created Adam, the ingredient was the dust that would have been moistened by the "mist (that) went up from the earth and watered the whole face of the ground." (Genesis 2:6) So, God made man out of mud—a mud cake baked in the heat of the Holy Spirit that had hovered over the face of the water. (Genesis 1:2; NIV) The dust of the earth, the soil, in the Mesopotamian region, where (according to some biblical archeologists) the garden was located, is colored. Now, this is not a very strong argument, but if Noah was white and the other humans were not, then they were likely brown or dark skinned. This skin pigment would have been passed down from the product of the Genesis account, father of mankind (Adam), which would suggest that Adam was brown or dark skinned.[147]

But this brings up another provocative question—maybe the most controversial. Genesis 1:27 says, "So God created man in his own image." Hold it. Don't over spiritualize this to avoid the question. Don't say, "Well it really means man had feelings like God. It means man can talk like God. It means man can think like God." No, no, no. Let's not play the spiritualize card here. Yes, all that stuff is true, but Adam had a body. Adam had arms and legs. Adam had a face. And Adam's face had to look like *something*. It had to have some sort of color, shade, or hue. Don't tell me that doesn't matter now. I get it in terms of salvation and even in terms of the great love of God. But the man had to look like something. Adam had to have had a color. I will even give you that Adam was an earth-realm image of the invisible spirit-realm creator God. I've got that. But whatever He made and whatever Adam looked like, it was wrapped up in *skin that had to have some color.*

As some do when New Testament questions are left hanging without a cultural, contextual historical answer, we go to a Josephus to help us fill in the blanks—without taking away the spiritual truth revelation but enhancing the existential understanding of it.

---

147  Ibid.

I offer the extra-biblical, filler-in of the blanks, the Book of Enoch. And I suggest Lamech was a black man who had an albino-type baby, Noah, whose parents were people of color, with parents of color, with parents of color, all the way back to parents called Adam and Eve—a man and woman of color who were made in the image of their creator God. And what does that say about God? Why question this "theory" presented and supported with the same principles of biblical research and interpretation that have been passed down through the ages, but all controlled and passed down by white scholars, white theologians, white academicians?

Have you closed this book and put it down yet? If so, if any of this rubs you the wrong way, if it raises your inquisitiveness and skepticism.... Now you know how I feel!

But. What. If. God on earth—this man Jesus—was black?

The walls come tumbling down. At least they should. But humans get involved, and their motives, their self-centeredness, build walls and divisions and racism and separation of that which God meant to be unified. As I've said a few times here, you have never been in a fight until you get into a fight with someone who feels God is on his or her side. It was that way in the Crusades. That's the way it was with historic holy wars in the name of Allah. That's the way it was with the Reformation. That's the way it was with slavery. That's the way it is with skinheads and white nationalists. That's the way it was with the KKK. But the question is not, is never going to be, "Is God on my side?" The question is and always will be, "Who's on the Lord's side?"

During the writing of this chapter, I taught a class on racism and reconciliation at The King's University in Dallas. Toward the end of the class, a tall millennium-type doctoral student came to me at the break. With tears in his eyes, he said, "Dr. Ulmer, this class has changed my life." As humbly as I could, I thanked him for taking the class and said, "Praise the Lord. I'm glad it's helping." He said, "No, you don't understand. I was a member of the Ku Klux Klan in Mississippi. You have no idea how this class has saved my life. Like you, I am a recovering racist!"

# 11

# COME TOGETHER

It was 1989. The giant social prophet and singer-songwriter John Lennon sounded the musical shofar in a time of social fragmentation and responded to a scene of what was deemed by the white drug subculture to be an injustice: the imprisonment of drug advocate Timothy Leary during his campaign for governor of California. The case was based on Leary's alleged possession of marijuana. Lennon's response as a musical artist was to call the nation to "Come Together." Lennon is reported to have said this about his creation of the song:

> "The thing was created in the studio. It's gobbledygook; 'Come Together' was an expression that Leary had come up with for his attempt at being president or whatever he wanted to be, and he asked me to write a campaign song. I tried and tried, but I couldn't come up with one. But I came up with this, 'Come Together,' which would've been no good to him—you couldn't have a campaign song like that, right?"[148]

This song would become a rallying cry for primarily white activists calling for sociological and cultural unity in their fractured existence. The lyrics, by Lennon's own label of the product as "gobbledygook," made little sense to listeners, but the simple melody and the profound exhortation of the song made it powerful. It was a call for reconciliation. A coming together.

---

148   Sheff, David; *All We Are Saying: The Last Major Interview with John Lennon and Yoko Ono*. New York. St. Martin's Press (2000) ISBN 0-312-25464-4. See: https://archive.org/details/allwearesayingla00lenn

Another unlikely painful call for "coming together" rose from the ashes of destruction, rage, and defiance in the wake of white policemen and black motorist Rodney King. It was a shivering voice at the center of the urban conflict, for Rodney King himself. On May 1, 1992, after the white policemen were acquitted of the beating of King, in the cloud, fog, and residue of riot smoke that evidenced widespread destruction, King appeared and appealed for calm, asking rhetorically and plaintively, "Can we all get along?" It was a call for calm. It was a call for peace in the battleground streets of South Central Los Angeles. It was a call for reconciliation.

This call, this exhortation, this challenge for reconciliation was part of the message of Paul the apostle in 2 Corinthians 5:16-21:

> "So, from now on we regard no one from a worldly point of view. Though we once regarded Christ in this way, we do so no longer. Therefore, if anyone is in Christ, he is a new creation; the old has gone, the new has come! All this is from God, who reconciled us to Himself through Christ and gave us the ministry of reconciliation: that God was reconciling the world to Himself in Christ, not counting men's sins against them. And He has committed to us the message of reconciliation. We are therefore Christ's ambassadors, as though God were making His appeal through us. We implore you on Christ's behalf: Be reconciled to God. God made Him who had no sin to be sin for us, so that in Him we might become the righteousness of God." (NIV)

Paul places the issue of reconciliation into a spiritual framework. When we turn to biblical references of reconciliation, we raise the discussion to a spiritual level that should not be divorced from the existential reality of the need for reconciliation.

The very concept and idea of reconciliation seems to have become a buzz word tossed about, albeit sincerely, but often watered down to a prayer meeting attended by those of differing theological positions, or an outward expression of repentance and humble regret of the status quo. In *Roadmap to Reconciliation: Moving Communities into Unity, Wholeness and Justice*, Brenda Salter McNeil put it this way:

> "Reconciliation has become a trendy topic of conversation ...which isn't necessarily a bad thing. People are talking about it, and that's good. There are gatherings, teachings, sermons, classes and entire conferences around the subject of reconciliation. But, if we're not careful, it is quite possible and tempting to be more in love with the idea of reconciliation than to actually engage in the actual work of reconciliation—the arduous, painful and messy marathon work of reconciliation. That's the pivotal question we must ask: Are we more in love with the idea of following Jesus than actually following Jesus—including to and through some difficult areas?"[149]

Without presenting an exhaustive exegesis on the biblical issue of reconciliation or drifting into philosophical debates on preferred methodologies of achieving reconciliation founded on biblical revelation, I have hoped to highlight a true personal dilemma that has challenged me whenever I try to bring this issue to my own life. I would highly recommend *Roadmap to Reconciliation* by Dr. Brenda Salter, *The Woke Church* by Dr. Eric Mason, and *Insider Outsider*, by my god-son, Bryan Loritts. These contemporary, scholarly, yet practical works, like a fine diamond with many flashing glints from the multiple faces of the same gem, will challenge, confront, and

---

149   McNeil, Brenda Salter. *Roadmap to Reconciliation: Moving Communities into Unity, Wholeness and Justice.* Downers Grove: IVP Books. 2015. Kindle Edition. Location 1879 of 1902.

empower you to change your perspective, participation and priority on this relevant social and spiritual issue.

Having lived for over seven decades both filled with and seasoned by the reality of racism, segregation, and racial oppression, I must deal with a painful reality: The truth is that reconciliation begins with *me*, on my side of the wall of division. The ball is in my court. I must make the first move. And this angers me. Frustrates me. And challenges me.

One frustration I often find myself facing is the difficulty of discussion. A conversation about race with my white friends is almost null and void. I agree with Robin DiAngelo that it is hard for white people to talk about racism. Dr. DiAngelo coins the term "white fragility" to describe the silence, defensiveness, argumentation, certitude, and other forms of pushback that are often manifested by white people regarding the topic of racism. She suggests these responses are not natural but are formed by social forces and restrict the potential, productive, helpful knowledge that can come forth from transparent, honest dialogue, and more times than not, function more powerfully to hold the racial hierarchy in place.[150] The commonly accepted concept of racism sees it as a label for immoral, mean people who intentionally dislike people because of their race or color.[151] However, in my experience, I would give most racists the benefit of the doubt and suggest that they more often than not "unintentionally" or at least subconsciously display racists practices. Few would openly admit to being racist. (Though many in these days fraught with angry political discourse go right up to the edge of stating it—though in disguised terminology— utilizing words such as "nationalism" and phrases like, "Go back where you came from," and "You don't belong here!")

150   DiAngelo, Robin J. *White Fragility*. Beacon Press. Kindle Edition; pg. 8 of 169. Location 349 of 2928.
151   Ibid.

I find an additional challenge with my black comrades in attempting to enter dialogues about race and racism. I have been in settings where I was an obvious dissenter of actions and positions that were contrary to the assumed party line of black America. In most circles of color where I traffic, it is assumed we are liberal or even leftist, often socialist, radical and boundlessly egalitarian. Hence my recurring internal, intimate, spiritual tug of war between my blackness and my Bible.

I did not realize the degree to which living in a time of often pervasive, sometimes more subtle, expressions of racism have impacted my life both positively and negatively. I am annoyed with myself when I hear a news report of some crime that has captured the headlines, and I realize that my first emotional reaction is not so much about the victim, or even the detailed nature of the crime, but my first gulp of air is heavy with the thought *I hope the perp wasn't black.*

On a more trivial, even petty level, I have caught myself wondering if some new face of black success is a person married to a white spouse. I have shrugged a disgusted shoulder of "shame on me" when I have tried to mask my irritation when I see a person of color exhibiting behavior, appearance, or attitude that feeds into stereotypes of non-compliance, non-conformist, or rebellion and think, "That's why we can't get ahead." I am growing out of such old-school thoughts, which is actually part of the residue of the need to be delivered from the infection of my own experiences, pain, and encounters with the realities of race.

Ultimately, I refuse to choose. I live my life in the accepted, welcomed, God-given tension between the two. I will not raise my flag of black identity and lower my shield as a soldier of the cross. I will not become so God-focused that I numb myself to the perpetual expressions of racism that plague these last days. I will never minimize the truth that I am, by the blood of Christ, a black son of the living God enshrouded in the blackness He gave me. I am not ashamed of the truth of God and Christ the Lord and Savior. I have deposited my faith in the love of God and the life of Christ. I refuse to allow the culture I have been assigned to live in to shape and mold and fashion me to comfortably fit into its restricted, warped pattern of thinking or living. I am who I am by the grace of God.

I am so grateful to God for my journey of healing. In the words of the old gospel song, "I've come a long way (in 70 years), but I still have a long way to go." I am secure in who I am and whose I am.

What shall we say, then, about these things? Let me clearly say that I have no pat answer to the complex issue of racism. I don't have a quick-fix formula to clear the cultural air of this demonic infestation. However, I do have a starting point. I believe we have been given at least three principles that form the foundation of a righteous response to any approach with the sanction, power, and authority of God.

These are all variations on the theme of the liberating love of God manifested as a many-faceted diamond of affirmation, acceptance, equality, and deliverance. These give us a theological framework for the mandate to be ambassadors of reconciliation. Paul is the primary revelator of the biblical concept of reconciliation. Brenda McNeil presents reconciliation as an "ongoing spiritual process involving forgiveness, repentance, and justice that restores broken relationships and systems to reflect God's original intention for all creation to flourish."[152]

Famed hymnist, pastor, and scholar Dr. Jack Hayford reveals the multi-dimensional dynamic of reconciliation:

> "Our relationship with God dictates our relationship
> with other people. God brought us out of a deep pit and
> showed us mercy and kindness. His grace should mirror

---

152   McNeil, Brenda Salter. *Roadmap to Reconciliation: Moving Communities into Unity, Wholeness and Justice.* Downers Grove: IVP Books. 2015. Kindle Edition. Location 194 of 1902.

through us to the world. You have to make the decision that you *want* to be reconciled to other people. You have to believe that Jesus can help you love a person for His sake. Human kindness will only get us so far, but the blood of Jesus has the power to transform us and bring new life to our relationships. We should approach people as Jesus did, as a servant who loves and cares for them. WE can't do this by ourselves; we need His Spirit. The life of Jesus comes through us by the ministry of reconciliation. When God reconciled us to Himself, He did not label us with our failures. He welcomed and accepted us despite all our shortcomings."[153]

Sin not only breaks our vertical relationship with God but also our horizontal relationship with others. Racism is sin. The only good thing about sin—if that is an allowable oxymoron—is that it can be forgiven, and the fractured relationship can be reconciled, put back together, repositioned in fellowship. I do not think this is a hyper-spiritualized utopian possibility. I believe it comes under the auspices of the "all things" that are possible through Christ. I feel like Dr. Martin Luther King, Jr., in that I may not live long enough to see it, but I believe the power of God can restore the brokenness that characterizes His created humanity. I believe this based on three theologies. The theology of Peter, the Fisherman model. The theology of Paul, the Corinthian model. The theology of Bishop Desmond Tutu, the African model.

The theology of Peter the fisherman is a theology of revelation. The scene in the life of the fisherman in Acts chapter 10 becomes the foundational text that reveals biblical and theological validation of racial reconciliation. The text clearly has racial and cultural implications. Peter would learn that the love of God is able to scale

153  Hayford, Jack. "Why Can't We All Just Get Along?" *Fresh Start Bible: Direction for Every Day.* Southlake, TX: Gateway Press. 2019. P 1024.

racial, ethnic, and cultural walls as he would experience the power of God not only falling on the souls in the house of Cornelius, but on the house of a Gentile. The emphasis in the text is that this move of the Holy Spirit in trans-racial, and Peter the Jew sees the power of God in the life of a Gentile just as with the founders of the first church at Pentecost—Jews! (Acts 10:47)

Apostle Peter presents an approach to reconciliation based on his revelation of the non-discriminating nature of the love of God. We see this in the scene of the heavenly sheet with a variety of animals, many of which were considered unclean and off limits to any practicing Jew. After refusing to eat according to the law, the Lord declares that all He calls clean is—in fact—clean and edible. This revelation coupled with the manifestation of the power of the Holy Spirit crossing the line of demarcation into the life of a man named Cornelius and his family (Acts 10:9-35) leads Peter in the prophetic declaration, "I see very clearly that God shows no favoritism. In every nation He accepts those who fear Him and do what is right." The word for "nation" is the word "ethnos" from which we get our word ethnicity. This is "A multitude, people, race, belonging and living together."[154] Peter affirms that the love of God is both the demonstration and the exhortation upon which reconciliation is possible. In *What Does the Bible say about Racism?* noted best-selling author and Chancellor of The King's University, Robert Morris writes, "Racism and prejudice have no place in the Kingdom of God. Every single person, no matter their skin color, is made in His image."[155] Morris cites examples of the biblical position on racism:

---

154  *The Complete Word Study Dictionary: New Testament* © 1992 by AMG International, Inc. Revised Edition, 1993)

155  Morris, Robert. What Does the Bible say about Racism? *Fresh Start Bible.* P968.

Racism is pure evil. (Romans 12:9)
Racism is pure self-righteousness (Luke 18:11)
Racism violates the Great Commission (Matthew 28:19)
Racism violates the Great Commandment (John 13:34-35)
Racism questions God's creation (Acts 17:26)
Racism questions God's plan (Revelation 5:9)
Racism questions God (John 3:16)[156]

Peter, the big fisherman, learned that a true fisher of men shows no favoritism toward the variety of fish he is allowed to catch. The Fisherman model shows us that the net that God casts is wide enough to catch all species of human races, ethnicities, and even nations for the glory of God. The Fisherman model informs us that discrimination on the basis of external factors is wrong—especially for believers, who honor God, who is no respecter of persons. On the other hand, the Fisherman model teaches us something else. We see that the breakdown of racism can be a difficult possibility to accept. Peter the fisherman struggled with the will of God regarding equality. Maybe it is no wonder so many of us do also.

When we remember the extent of the Great Commission, we see a sequential relationship between the Fisherman model and the Corinthian model. Jesus said, "You shall receive power when the Holy Spirit comes upon you. And you will be my witnesses, telling people about me everywhere—in Jerusalem, through Judea, in Samaria, and to the ends of the earth." (Acts 1:8 NLT) The commission given to the church is, by definition, a call to breakdown and cross over walls. Jesus spoke these words to the disciples as they stood "in Jerusalem." Jerusalem, their home base. Jesus said, "You start here. You move into Judea." Judea is a geographical territory. The *Dictionary of New Testament Background* describes it like this:

---

156 Ibid.

"Judea: Comprising the regions immediately surrounding the city of Jerusalem, Judea encompassed the hill country and desert fringe dividing the Shephelah from the Dead Sea. Intermittently, during periods of Hasmonean, Herodian and Roman rule, "Judea" could also be used to designate the totality of regions controlled by Jerusalem's monarch or the Roman governor at Caesarea Maritima (see Roman Administration; Roman Governors of Palestine). At various times, these possessions included Idumea, Samaria, Galilee and portions of the Mediterranean coast and Transjordan."[157]

Taking the love of God from Jerusalem crosses geographical walls. However, Jesus goes on to say, "...Samaria." "Samaritans were a 'mixed race' contaminated by foreign blood and false worship."[158] "In NT times the Samaritans were a substantial religious group inhabiting parts of the central hill country of Samaria between Galilee to the north and Judea to the south, but with Diaspora communities in addition."[159] The Samaritan phase of Kingdom expansion would cross geographical and ethnic walls. Clearly, "...the ends of the earth," or as the good King Jim calls it "...the uttermost part of the world," (KJV) indicates breaking down racial walls into the land of the Gentiles. "Gentiles" was a term that meant, in its simplest form, non-Jews: "The Heb. (goi) and Greek (ethnos) words denote invariably a nation or a people, never a person."[160]

As we have seen, the word "ethnos" is used also for nations

---

157  *Dictionary of New Testament Background*, edited by Craig A. Evans and Stanley E. Porter, © 2000 by InterVarsity Christian Fellowship/USA. Published by InterVarsity Press. All rights reserved. No part may be reproduced without written permission from InterVarsity Press, P.O. Box 1400, Downers Grove, IL 60515 or permissions@ivpress.com.)

158  *Nelson's Illustrated Bible Dictionary*, Copyright © 1986, Thomas Nelson Publishers

159  *Dictionary of New Testament Background*; edited by Craig A. Evans and Stanley E. Porter, © 2000 by InterVarsity Christian Fellowship/USA. Published by InterVarsity Press. All rights reserved. No part may be reproduced without written permission from InterVarsity Press, P.O. Box 1400, Downers Grove, IL 60515 or permissions@ivpress.com.)

160  *Hastings' Dictionary of the Bible: One-volume Edition.* Biblesoft formatted electronic database. Copyright © 2015 by Biblesoft, Inc. All rights reserved.

and refers to those who were not Jews in any and all terms: religiously, ethnically, or racially. For Paul and elsewhere in the NT it is used to refer to nations other than the nation of Israel. The message that God now accepts men and women from all nations into full covenant relationship without the need for conversion to Judaism is an insight given supremely to Paul and one which threatened deep splits within the early church.[161]

The Pauline concept of reconciliation is developed in his second letter to the Corinthians, in 2 Corinthians 5:17-21:

> "Therefore, if anyone is in Christ, he is a new creation; the old has gone, the new has come! All this is from God, who reconciled us to Himself through Christ and gave us the ministry of reconciliation: that God was reconciling the world to Himself in Christ, not counting men's sins against them. And He has committed to us the message of reconciliation. We are therefore Christ's ambassadors, as though God were making His appeal through us. We implore you on Christ's behalf: Be reconciled to God. God made Him who had no sin to be sin for us, so that in Him we might become the righteousness of God." (NIV)

Paul's idea of the power of God is to make any who follow Christ "new creations" but also calls us into the ministry assignment of being instruments, ministers, servants—even ambassadors of reconciliation with the job description of crossing boundaries, walls, and divisions that separate men from God and men from each other. Paul's instruction, coupled with the extent of the commission of Jesus, requires crossing geographical, ethnic, religious, racial—all—walls of separation, all boundaries of distinction and lines of demarcation. As the Fisherman model is one of revelation, the

---

161   *Dictionary of Paul and His Letters* © 1993 by InterVarsity Christian Fellowship/USA. All rights reserved.

Corinthian model is one of renewal based on the inclusiveness of
new creation as a demonstration of the love of God that crosses all
boundary lines and breaks down all walls.

My life was changed by two significant trips. My first visit
to Israel brought me back to my spiritual roots. My first visit to
South Africa brought me back to my ethnic roots. I visited South
Africa two months after Dr. Nelson Mandela was released from
prison in 1990. My prize possession is a picture of him and me in
his backyard. Four years later, in 1994, he would be elected the
first black president of South Africa marking the beginning of the
demise of the demonic political system of apartheid. His platform
for election emphasized the need for racial reconciliation in the
broken nation of South Africa. This value was translated into
the Truth and Reconciliation Commission (TRC) lead by His
Grace Archbishop Desmond Tutu. This mighty giant (Actually,
physically he was a small giant.) forged an effort to bring healing
to the racially-battered nation. This Anglican cleric was driven by
a historical call for victims to confront those who had committed
violence against them—face to face.

Then Bishop Tutu moved under divine mandate to break
down the barriers that divided his multi-tribal predominantly
black homeland which was but previously dominated by the white
minority. It is this scenario that presents us with the African model
of reconciliation. The Bishop brought to reconciliation a theology
of race. This powerful indigenous Theo-philosophy was a unique
synthesis of biblical, liberation, and African theologies that valued
the individual as a necessary and mandatory unit of corporate unity
and oneness. This African model is based on a theo-philosophy
that is peculiarly and particularly non-Western. It is germane to
this discussion to point out that American racism is the fruit of a
broader, older Westernized mindset. Dr. Robin DiAngelo posits

that the core of racism in America is founded in the Western ideology of individualism and objectivity:

> "Individualism is a story line that creates, communicates, reproduces, and reinforces the concept that each of us is a unique individual and that our group memberships, such as race, class, or gender, are irrelevant to our opportunities. Individualism claims that there are no intrinsic barriers to individual success and that failure is not a consequence of social structures but comes from individual character. According to the ideology of individualism, race is irrelevant."[162]

Bishop Tutu brings African theology and cultural tradition based on this theology front and center in his reconciliation model. This concept is called "Ubuntu." From Michael Battle suggests in *Ubuntu: I in You and You in Me*,

> "The African person's understanding of spirituality brings to the Western person sacred relationship and the experience of harmony with nature, a lack of domineering attitude toward nature, a sense of the invisible world alive in the visible, and a strong conviction that various spirits can communicate with the person and the community. These African understandings challenge Western perceptions of the secularity of the universe, a sense of control over it, and a great skepticism about the existence of any kinds of spirits or similar beings with power to influence human behavior notwithstanding the contributions of modern psychology, which has shown us that we are far more complex than we have dreamed. Within this complexity we are then

---

162  DiAngelo, Robin J. *White Fragility* (p. 10). Beacon Press. Kindle Edition.

led to the African understandings of Ubuntu. The reader learns that in many respects, the concept of Ubuntu as interpersonality sums up the way African individuality and freedom are always balanced by the destiny of the community...Ubuntu does not presuppose that individuals lose their particularity, but it never loses sight of their place in the whole."[163]

Tutu places African theology as the model for reconciliation and acknowledges that is it contra-Western in its grounding. This is Ubuntu. Battle writes, "Ubuntu can offer Western Christian spirituality communal practices of God's presence that inform how a person moves beyond Western definitions of spirituality that are often self-contained with little understanding of relationality."[164] Ubuntu, the African contribution to the ministry of reconciliation, is grounded in the plan of God (Gen. 1:27), the prayer of Jesus on His way to Calvary (John 17:20-22), and the plea of Paul (Eph. 3:17-19). The plan of God was to create man male and female and unite them as one demonstration of the image of God. Jesus prayed that the disciples would be unified in oneness, demonstrating the diversity in the unity of the godhead. Finally, Paul prays that the saints would know the dimensions of the love of God but clarifies that they can only know this multi-dimensional love to the degree that they are one with one another.

> John 17:20-22: "My prayer is not for them alone. I pray also for those who will believe in me through their message, that all of them may be one, Father, just as you are in me and I am in you. May they also be in us so that the world may believe that you have sent me." (NIV)

---

163   Battle, Michael. *Ubuntu: I in You and You in Me.* Church Publishing Inc. Kindle Edition. Location 1205, 1195 of 210.
164   Ibid. Location 1234 of 2106.

Ubuntu is found in the plan of God, the prayer of Christ, and the plea of Paul. African traditional concept of Ubuntu breeds an "African epistemology that) begins with community and moves to individuality, whereas Western epistemology moves from individuality to community."[165] In Battle's *Ubuntu*, Bishop Tutu concludes:

> "[God] has chosen us to be his partners, therefore everything he does with us is theandric—both divine and human. God chooses to limit Himself according to our limitations, to make of Himself a 'weak' God. In his relationship with us his divine omnipotence is conditioned by our human weakness."[166]

The Bishop uses the oppressive political reality of his own dear South Africa as an antithetical example of the truth of God's love for man. "Apartheid says people are created for separation, people are created for apartheid, people are created for alienation and division, disharmony and disunity, and we say, the Scripture says, people are made for togetherness, people are made for fellowship."[167]

The African Ubuntu reveals the mind of God, the method demonstrated by the love of Christ and the model for crashing through the walls of racism. Ubuntu affirms the value and necessity of forgiveness as part of the process of reconciliation. "Forgiveness can be experienced not only as a gift given, but as a gift received. The very term 'forgiveness' is built on the root 'give.'" Forgiveness is a symbol, a sacrament of one's conviction of the givenness of life. In the act of forgiving, believers imitate God. Forgiveness is a creative act that changes us from prisoners of the past.[168]

Here is the practical, spiritual challenge for believers and it puts the reconciliation ball in our court. The necessity and

---

165    Ibid. Location 1841 of 2106.
166    Ibid. Location 587 of 2106.
167    Ibid. Location 1157 of 2106.
168    Ibid. Location 1999 of 2106.

requirement of forgiveness as an element of racial reconciliation is frightening to the victims of racism. It implies that we are called to forgive the racists. The problem is that we call upon our loving God to "...Forgive us as we forgive those who trespass against us." Wow. Lord, forgive me as—in the same manner as I forgive those who have victimized me through wretched racism. But, Lord, you forgive me before I ask to be forgiven. You are eternally ready to receive my prayer for forgiveness—*before I even ask.*

So, am I supposed to be the one to make the first step? Am I to really forgive the racist? Am I to expect you to forgive me in the same way, in the same manner, in the same timing that I forgive the racist? Lord, forgive me of my sins in the same way I forgive the racists who have sinned against me?

Lord, have mercy.

We have marching orders. We are called into duty to serve in the army of the Lord as soldiers fighting for righteousness and rightness. We are called to break down the walls of division that desecrate the will and the way of the Divine. We are armed with the inspiration of the Fisherman model of revelation of God whose love does not play favorites. We have seen the Corinthian model of the new, creative power of the love of God that unites us to spread the news and truth of His love as agents of reconciliation.

Finally, we are called to emulate the African model that we are one together. "Christian spirituality can be genuinely personal only to the extent that it is practiced communally. It is recognizable and intelligible only when it relates fully to one's neighbor."[169]

---

169  Ibid. Location 2003 of 2106.

# 12

# EPILOGUE

What then shall we conclude after having reasoned together in more than 200 pages on racism? Is it an utterly unsolvable dilemma in the physical earth realm as long as human beings are involved? I can't say.

But what I can say is that racism is not a one-dimensional, monolithic reality of the modern world. It is a multi-faceted, ideological construct that is fluid—but fluid in its rigidity. Its expressions vary within cultural contexts, but it rigidly defends and passionately maintains its hierarchy of white supremacy and superiority.

Racism is a systemic, institutional, historic, cultural mindset. Most of all, it is a wall builder. It is a constructed system of seemingly unbreachable walls and uncrossable lines. This ideology of superiority is most often a twin pillar of a matching theology processed by an erroneously godless hermeneutic. As a believer in both the truth and the power of the Word of God, I must revert to a faith that admittedly is often fragile and spiritually flawed, but ever faithful. I refuse to comfortably lie down on my side of the base of the wall. I declare and decree: These walls can fall. I don't have a program. I don't have a printable, portable process. Sorry. Right now, all I have is the faith that walls can fall. I am frustrated by that fact. I am exasperated because my ego and pride say I should have an answer. I should have a 12-step program to remove racism. I should have a therapeutic exercise that will excise it. I should have a 10-point plan for eradicating it. I don't.

In fact, if you have a guaranteed resolution or a fail-proof demolition strategy, then I encourage you write it down and publish it. I am satisfied that if you have read this work this far so that God can give you a revelation, a prophetic utterance, a tactical technique of wall demolition, then you should join me and shout it out: *Walls can fall!*

I am not discouraged or daunted in my mantra "Walls can fall," by past attempts, fueled by high expectations and seasoned with prayer petitions, which have only produced undetected, or immeasurable success in chipping away at the wall.

I have attended reconciliation rallies and reconciliation worship services. I will not wash any more feet. I won't sit any more in humble, embarrassing postures of submission while timidly extending my own feet to be tenderly and nervously publicly washed. Been there, done that, got the tee shirt and the hat. I say this not at all to denigrate such sincere positively motivated pseudo-spiritual calisthenics. It's just that I have tried it, and I have seen it tried by others. And usually—admittedly, not definitively "never"—but usually such public displays of repentance, regret, and restart have produced two results: little and none. And most often, when the feet and towels have dried, the same feet march back to business as usual. Even in the face of such demonstrations of drive-by kneel-down sincerity, the wall still stands, albeit defaced by scratches of such short-lived events.

Please know that I don't make such observations as a scrooge-type killjoy with a rain-on-the-parade attitude toward such sincere steps. It is just that the miniscule cracks in the wall of racism do not deter or deflate my conviction that the walls can fall.

The Emancipation Proclamation did not drop the walls. The legislated end of slavery did not drop the walls. The life-sacrificing efforts of the Abolitionists did not drop the walls. The tear-stained trails of the Freedom Riders did not drop the walls. The almost monthly gun-downs of blacks by whites, year after year, and the attendant righteous anger and tearful indignation of the masses have produced nothing. Sit-ins, pray-ins, marches and demonstrations have come and gone. They have been reincarnated through the "Matter Movements" with variations on the same thematic diagnosis, as Lonnae O'Neal wrote in a 2017 article in *The Undefeated*:

> The Blue Lives Matter (*the problem is violent black people*), Black Lives Matter (*the problem is the criminal justice system, poor training and police bias*) and All Lives Matter (*the problem is police and black people*) arguments are extensions of the same, three-way debate (*segregationist, anti-racist and assimilationist*) that Americans have been having since the founding of the country.[170]

I am excited by the progress of a new generation of wall blasters like Ibram Kendi, founder of the Antiracist Research and Policy Center at American University and a brilliant creative millennial historian, who takes an institutional approach to bringing down the institutional wall of racism. This gifted scholar proposes an innovative strategy involving a wall-dropping intellectual team of academicians, researchers, and other scholars, whose goal is to "identify inequalities, identify the policies that create and maintain those inequalities, and propose correctives in six areas: criminal justice, education, economics, health, environment and politics."[171] Kendi is driven by his creative version of the belief that these walls can fall. To this rising lieutenant in the army of the righteous, I say, "Welcome to the war." Go for it. I, too, believe it. Walls *can* fall.

I have been a part of movements that targeted—at least

---

170   O'Neal, Lonnae; September 20, 2017, article in "The Undefeated" titled "Ibram Kendi, The Nation's Leading Scholars on Racism, says, Education and Love are not the answer." See: https://theundefeated.com/features/ibram-kendi-leading-scholar-of-racism-says-education-and-love-are-not-the-answer/

171   Ibid.

philosophically—racism, with varying degrees of success, whatever practical success is. We have not yet arrived. We have come a long way, but we obviously still have a long way to go. We have kicked the wall. We have prayed at the wall. We have anointed the wall with oil. We have marched, up and down, back and forth; we have marched around the wall seeking cracks, crevices, breaks in it, and weak spots in it. We have blasted it with the dynamite of determination. We have tried to bring it down with flames of faith, and yet it remains. Maybe that's a hint: No matter what the strategy, it will require, it will demand, it will necessitate the power of steadfast faith that *it will fall*.

That's where I'm coming from. I believe walls can fall. I join with the father of the mentally ill boy, in confessional repentance flowing from a heart with a hunger and thirst to see a demonstration of the powerful object of his flickering faith. Hear my prayer, Oh Lord:

"Lord I believe, help my unbelief." (Mark 9:16 KJV) Hear my prayer, Oh Lord. I have faith, but I need more. I join the ranks of the embarrassed disciples who were challenged to release unimaginable unmeasurable forgiveness with the prayerful plea, "Lord, increase our faith." Lord, that kind of forgiveness requires a little more faith than I have. But my faith in not in my faith, Lord, my faith is in you. And so, Lord, by faith I believe these walls can fall. I believe you can erase the lines of racial boundaries, restricted justice, and inequality. I know it is not a quick fix or calculated formula. Father, give me faith ability to see over the walls. Give me the spiritual x-ray vision to see through the walls. Give me bulldozer faith to push through the walls. Give me forward march faith to march right through the walls. Give me upward faith to fix my eyes over the walls and gaze at your glory. Give me forgetful faith to forget the pain of my past inflicted by agents of racist mindlessness. Give me love faith to love the wall builders and guards committed to the extension of the walls. Give me knowing faith that knows walls don't fall by "might or by power, but by (your) Spirit." Give me handshake faith to reach out and clutch white hands that represent ages of tireless grips of discriminating, oppressive power. Lord, give me time, give me the days, give me the years to stand by faith in the dust of fallen walls of racism. And yet, Lord, I stand firm in my faith confession: The walls of racism *can* fall. I walk by faith like Joshua around the perimeters of the prohibitive walls, and I declare these walls can fall. Bring them down, Lord. Make them fall, Lord. Falling walls are not impossible with you. Almighty Wall-Dropper bring down the walls of racism, bigotry, and injustice. Use me, Oh Lord, as a wall dropper. Strengthen my voice so that I may shout it like the piercing tones of the shofar and the blast of a hallowed horn: The walls of racism can come down. Walls can fall.

Amen. And they *will*, God willing.

# ABOUT THE AUTHOR

Dr. Kenneth C. Ulmer is Senior Pastor of Faithful Central Bible Church in Southern California. He participated in the study of ecumenical liturgy and worship at Magdalen College at Oxford University in England. He has served as an instructor in pastoral ministry and homiletics at Grace Theological Seminary, as an instructor of African-American preaching at Fuller Theological Seminary in Pasadena, as an adjunct professor at Biola University (where he served on the board of trustees), and as an adjunct professor at Pepperdine University. He is past president of The King's University, Dallas, Texas, founded by Dr. Jack Hayford; he is also a founding board member and currently an adjunct professor at The King's. For over two decades, he has served as Director of The King's at Oxford (a summer session of The King's University held at Oxford University, United Kingdom). He has served as mentor in the Doctor of Ministry Degree programs at United Theological Seminary and presently at Payne Theological Seminary.

Pastor Ulmer received his Bachelor of Arts degree in broadcasting and music from the University of Illinois and is a life member of the board of directors of The Gospel Music Workshop of America. After accepting his call to the ministry, he was ordained at Mount Moriah Missionary Baptist Church in Los Angeles and shortly afterward founded Macedonia Bible Baptist Church in San Pedro, California. He has studied at Pepperdine University, Hebrew Union College, the University of Judaism, Christ Church, and Magdalen College at Oxford University in England. He earned a Ph.D. from Grace Graduate School of Theology in Long Beach, California (later to become the West Coast Campus of Grace Theological Seminary). He also earned a Doctor of Ministry degree from United Theological

Seminary and was awarded an honorary Doctor of Divinity degree from Southern California School of Ministry.

In 1994, Dr. Ulmer was consecrated Bishop of Christian Education and founding member of the Bishops Council of the Full Gospel Baptist Church Fellowship. He is also Presiding Bishop over the Macedonia International Bible Fellowship, with includes churches representing South Africa, Great Britain, and the US. Bishop Ulmer serves as Co-Chair of Global Leaders Network, and Co-Chair of Empowered 21, an organization that is helping shape the future of the Spirit-empowered movement throughout the world by focusing on crucial issues facing the movement and connecting generations for intergenerational blessing and impartation.

Bishop Ulmer has written several books, including *Passing The Generation Blessing, A New Thing, Spiritually Fit to Run the Race, In His Image* (an update of his book *The Anatomy of God), Making Your Money Count, Knowing God's Voice, Passionate God*, and several others.

Married for 36 years, Dr. Ulmer and his wife are residents of Los Angeles, California, and have three daughters, one son, and six grandchildren.